# Breaking Glass

## Acknowledgements

I would like to acknowledge the assistance given so unselfishly by Mrs Anne Strain and to the Shankill Road Mission team for encouraging me to write this book. Also the Revd. J. Matthews and George Averley for their love and devotion to my family.

# Breaking Glass

## Eric Lennon

### with
### David Lee

Marshall Pickering

Marshall Morgan and Scott
Marshall Pickering
3 Beggarwood Lane, Basingstoke, Hants, RG23 7LP, UK

Copyright © 1987 by Eric Lennon and David Lee
First published by Marshall Morgan and Scott Publications Ltd
Part of the Marshall Pickering Holdings Group
A subsidiary of the Zondervan Corporation

Reprint : Impression number
87 88 89 90 : 10 9 8 7 6 5 4 3 2

**British Library CIP Data**

Lennon, Eric
  Breaking glass.
  I. Christian life
  I. Title    II. Lee, David, *1957–*
  248.4    BV4501.2
  ISBN 0-551-01447-4

Text set in Plantin by Brian Robinson, Buckingham
Printed in Great Britain by Hazell Watson & Viney Ltd,
Member of the BPCC Group, Aylesbury, Bucks.

# Contents

## Dedication

To my wife Olive and my family Heather, Isobel, Clifford and Geoffrey who suffered so much because of my alcoholism and lived to see their prayers answered.

# Foreword

Early in 1982 at the Shankill Road Mission we were looking for a man, a committed Christian who could get alongside the young men and women of the tortured inner city of Belfast where unemployment runs high and family breakdown and mindless violence are all too common. We advertised, held two sets of interviews, and finally agreed unanimously on Eric Lennon. He is a big rough-diamond of a man, an ex-alcoholic who has been in prison, a man who often appears aggressive, a man of drive. His record was bad, his life had been reckless and rebellious until one day in a terrible crisis when he was seeking to destroy himself, God in his amazing mercy intervened and rescued him.

And now, at interview, six years after this crisis, Eric sat before us. He was still going through a process of being cut down by God, a painful pruning, being made ready for some great work God had for him. This book tells his story up to that point.

A new work of God has started over these last years in the Shankill area, largely through the clear vision which God gave to Eric. It has started in a quiet way and it is growing. As God continued to knock rough edges off him (and some of the rest of us!) so Eric has been instrumental in showing a number of young men and women of this tragic and lost generation the real possibility of an utterly new kind of life in Jesus Christ.

He has been a good colleague and friend to me. We have been through hardship and blessing together. We have seen the Lord work a remarkable healing in Olive, his wife, something very lovely after all the years of anguish she has gone through. Olive today in her quiet way is still behind Eric and very supportive of him in the work.

Eric was at first very hesitant to publish this book. He is genuinely a man who shuns the limelight, recognising its dangers. Indeed God has given him a most precious gift – a deep humility – as a foundation for his many other gifts. But he became convinced that this story could be effective in pointing the way to hope – hope which does not fail, hope in the Lord Jesus Christ – for many who are caught and held in the severe grip of a hopeless addiction. I strongly commend this book to them and pray that they too in God's amazing mercy may reach out and receive this great salvation.

The Revd. Bill Jackson
Superintendent
Shankill Road Mission

February 1987

# 1: A visit

The walls were painted bright yellow, but no one had hung any pictures. Through the tiny hole that served as window and airvent came the sound of men playing football in the yard. If I'd stood on the edge of the bed I could have watched them, but I didn't move: someone would be coming to collect me for work in a few minutes and I didn't want to be caught spectating. Instead I lay with my hands behind my head and my eyes on the yellow ceiling, and waited. You did a lot of waiting around here.

Footsteps paused outside the door and the peephole shutter slid back.

'Lennon.'

I stood up. 'Yes?'

'You've got a visitor.'

The shutter closed and a key was inserted heavily into the lock. The door swung open to reveal the expressionless face of duty officer Smith.

'Who is it?'

'Just walk, Lennon.'

'Visits are in the afternoon.'

'I know.'

Suddenly he leaned forward with a strained ventriloquist's grin and added, 'It's not me who gives the orders, I'm only fetching you. Now move it.'

We descended the iron staircase half way along B Wing and proceeded to the Circle, where two prisoners were preparing to 'bump' the floor. Everything ran regular as clockwork in prison, and an unscheduled visit could only mean something was up. I wondered if it was Olive and the kids; Olive had been trying for some time to get my sentence reduced by petition – it could be she'd finally persuaded the police to sign, saying I wasn't a danger to society, and that I'd be let out sooner than I thought. But if that was the case she'd hardly have made a special visit. I was due to see her tomorrow anyway.

The visitors' block was a low wooden building arranged like a tennis court. Prisoners entered at one end, family and friends at the other; they conversed across a five foot counter with a thick wire grille running down the centre. You couldn't touch. It was hard even to see the person on the other side. And, of course, you couldn't expect privacy even with your wife. I was bracing myself for such an encounter when Smith turned away from the visitors' block and led me towards the prison offices. He let me into the governor's reception room. In contrast to the rest of the prison this was comfortably furnished with armchairs, carpets and wallpaper, even a vase of flowers. I stared dumbly as Smith withdrew, closing the door after him.

'Mr Lennon?'

A middle-aged clergyman had risen and was extending his hand to me. I took it.

'My name is McBride.'

'Yes?'

'I'm afraid I have some rather bad news for you.'

'Is this about the petition?'

'No. I think you'd better sit down.'

I obeyed. McBride crossed his fingers and went on in a quieter voice: 'I mean news of the worst possible kind. Your father died last night.'

Three, perhaps four seconds elapsed. He waited to see if I would say anything, and when I didn't, proceeded to supply the details. His voice seemed to be coming from the next room.

'. . .a cerebral hemorrhage. By all accounts it was very swift. He complained of having a headache, and a couple of minutes later he was gone. There can have been little pain.'

'My mother?' I heard myself saying.

'Your family are taking care of her. She was with him at the end.'

'How is she?'

'As well as can be expected. It's never easy.'

'I don't understand it. He was only sixty-two . . .'

'Yes, it is a tragedy. I am deeply sorry.'

'I take it you'll attend to the funeral. I mean, I can't . . .'

'Of course. It will be the day after tomorrow. In the circumstances I imagine parole will be a formality.'

I took a deep breath and looked down at the floor.

'If there's anything I can do, I'm available.'

'Yes. Thank you.'

'Your sister attends my church, so naturally I've heard some of what passed between you and your father.'

I nodded.

'Death can be a time for reconciliation. You mustn't blame yourself for all that's happened. I'm sure he wouldn't have wanted that.'

'Perhaps not. It's too late now.'

'If you give it time . . .'

I stood up, turning away, and remained for a moment with my arms folded. 'I'm sorry,' I said at last.

'I understand.'

'He was here three days ago, that's all. He came to ask me to go straight, go back to my wife . . .' I shrugged.

'And . . .?'

'And . . .I didn't even say goodbye.'

McBride didn't reply. I stared blankly at the window. Eventually he rose, we shook hands again and he left. Two days later, June 10th, 1965, I was in the funeral party watching my father's coffin lowered into the ground. I had mixed emotions. McBride had been right in saying I blamed myself – if not for his death then at least for the pain that preceded it – and I regretted missing my chance to put that right. But I also blamed him. In dying he had now received whatever reward it was his faith promised him; it was I who had to go on and pick up the broken pieces of a life. Perhaps it sounds strange for a son to blame his failures, his alcoholism and his criminal record on the conscientious faith of his father, but to my mind that was exactly how things stood, and in all fairness there is some truth in it. But then, every alcoholic loves a scapegoat.

# 2: Playing ball

I cycled home furiously, abandoning the bike next to the graceful tiled surround Father had mounted at the front door. The living room into which it opened was empty, though an unfinished cup of tea still sat on the piano. He'd probably been playing hymns.

'Mother!'

'Eric, don't shout so.'

My mother's head appeared from the tiny kitchen. 'Come in here if you want to say something.'

'Where's Father?'

'He's in the bedroom.'

'What's he doing?'

'Getting ready for the garden. Don't you ever stop asking questions?'

She took a stack of dinner plates down from the cupboard, laid them on the table and went to the cutlery drawer.

'Out of the way.'

'Mother, can I go to Lurgan this afternoon?'

'Now why would you want to go to Lurgan?'

'I need a brake cable.'

'And whose bike are you mending this time?'

'Harold's.'

'Well, there's a funny thing! I saw Harold yesterday and his bicycle looked good as new.'

'Mother! I need to go.'

11

She stopped her work to run a hand through my hair.

'You're sure you're not going to the football, Eric?'

'No.'

'A likely story.'

'Won't you ask Father?'

'Your father wouldn't approve. Besides, he'll want your help in the garden this afternoon.'

'Oh!' I whined. 'But Bill's going. All my chums are going.'

She laughed lightly, and began putting out the cutlery again. 'Such lies. You ought to be ashamed of yourself, Eric Lennon.'

'Just ask him. Please.'

'I will not. And nor will you,' she added, throwing me a warning glance.

'Eric!'

This time it was my father's voice. In a moment he was in the doorway, a thin, wiry man in rolled-up sleeves and a collarless shirt.

'There you are. Are you ready?'

I was aware of my mother's eyes resting on me, and of her relief when I replied dutifully, 'Yes, Father.'

Five minutes later I was out pumping water. What we called the garden was in fact a small market garden, one acre of land nearly half of which was covered by an enormous glasshouse. When I was very small Father had managed it single-handed; now that I'd come of age, if I wasn't at school or armed with an adequate excuse, I would be commandeered to help him. The round of work was endless, and seemed to intensify in the spring. Today after I'd finished watering in the glasshouse Father set me to work weeding the scallion bed. As I got down on my haunches and began yanking out the weeds I could see Father and my sister, Mary, talking as they worked in towards me from the opposite end.

I had reached that age when a child realises his own and his parent's wishes do not always coincide and begins, tentatively, to assert himself. That was why Harold's bike had so suddenly and inexplicably developed a faulty brake cable. But these little subterfuges always fell short of outright confrontation. I might have disobeyed my father if I thought I could get away with it, but I would never dream of challenging his authority with a request, for instance, to see the Glenavon match at Lurgan. He simply did not approve, and if Father disapproved of something it followed that you did not ask to do it.

'You're right, Mary. And in the Book of Joshua . . .' I heard him say from the other end of the scallion bed.

He was such a complex man for one you'd at first think so transparently simple. He didn't disapprove of football because it was bad for you, or because you might break your leg playing it. He said it was worldly and iniquitous, and that the mere act of spectating was the first step on a path leading inexorably to bondage in sin and eternal damnation. Everyone in the assembly we worshipped at took this view, and they were zealous for one another's improvement. Perhaps it was this vigilance that made my father so frugal in his pleasures and so austere in his relations with his family.

And yet there was a totally different side to him, for only a few months before when I'd been in hospital with suspected polio he had sat at my bedside day and night. No one could have shown more concern at my distress or plain joy when the condition was diagnosed as sunstroke and I was allowed to come home. No sooner was I cleared by the doctor than he swept me up in his arms and brought me back in the bicycle carrier, as proud a father as you ever saw. He didn't even stop to collect my clothes! But occasions like these were rare – glimpses of

13

a love so well · hidden that, most of the time, he himself hardly knew where to find it. I wondered what had made him like that.

Most people in the village of Donacloney had worked in the factory, and Father was no exception. The Donacloney mill was one of dozens set up by English entrepreneurs who had come over in the sixteenth century, saw that Irish land was good for flax, and set themselves up as Linen Lords. Even at my early age I understood that the power these men exercised over their workforce fell little short of tyranny. They built the factories and the houses and in return the people licked their boots. It was a simple matter of economic dependence. If you wanted to earn money and have a roof over your head you went out of your way to ingratiate yourself to your employer. You did it, according to Father, even when he refused to pay you at the end of the week because you hadn't got out your cut of cloth. I dimly understood his feelings about that period. There was no mercy. Father had been dismissed from his job at the factory, and evicted the same week. He had moved to a half-derelict cottage outside the village, renovated it with his own hands, and taken on work he could not have relished – as a salesman.

Apart from this memory the clearest influence on my father was his faith. Both he and my mother had been staunch members of the Donacloney Church of Ireland until in 1923 an itinerant evangelist passed through the area, leaving in his wake a crowd of converts to extreme biblical fundamentalism. Two features characterised the group. First their dedication to the Book – the Bible – and second, their growing intolerance of Anglicanism. It wasn't long before they were refusing to teach the catechism at Sunday school, and erected a wooden hut in the village (bought by Father for £32) to worship in on Sunday nights. Though, strictly speaking, it was inter-denominational the new congregation soon developed strong leanings towards the Brethren movement, and finally became a fully-fledged Brethren assembly. It could not have been to my father's liking – since he loved music and had taught the choir at the Anglican church – to see the organ removed from the gospel hall he had paid to put up.

It was this new, sterner phase in the church's life to which I was introduced. Without a doubt the most trying of the three weekly meetings was the Bible study. The principle of taking the Bible one book at a time was a sound one, but the assembly worked over the text with such laborious precision that it often took them two hours to cover a single verse. From this exercise they derived no practical benefit whatever, and nor did I. The meeting was a sort of shooting gallery for the congregation – almost none of whom had a higher than primary school education – to fire off quotations from whatever books and commentaries they had collected during the week. My only consolation was that this seemingly high-flown discussion produced some spectacular gaffes. Expounding the verse from Revelation that says 'The elements shall be dissolved in fervent heat', one man, who wouldn't have known an element if it stood up and hit him, clutched at the nearest interpretation and decided it must have four legs and a trunk. 'Just think,' he said soberly. 'All those big animals melting in the heat!' I had to stuff a handkerchief in my mouth to keep from laughing.

At the same time the meetings I'd known in my childhood had often been wonderful, and in my uncomplicated way I felt that I'd been brought into the

15

very presence of God. And if the Bible studies only occasionally rose from the ridiculous to the sublime the brethren were nonetheless far from naive. Like everyone in the area they had a dry wit. For instance, a speaker came one Sunday to preach on the Wilderness Journey of the Israelites. Though he waxed eloquent on the virtues of poverty and trust in God it was clear he wasn't exactly on the breadline himself, and as he was climbing back into his Jaguar one of the congregation who was leaning against the wall outside remarked in a loud voice, 'That camel'll not be troubled by too many stones in his hooves!'

All in all Christianity seemed a demanding faith. While other people in the village competed for material things, members of the assembly competed for mastery of dogma, and because this very often involved a detailed indent-ification of sins the competition was all the more fierce. It was at this point that the faith of the brothers who forbade flowers in church, and of the sisters who left their hair long, went beyond my grasp. What was it about football that made it a sin? Had God really ordained that kicking an inflated leather ball around qualified you for eternal damnation?

'Eric!'

I looked up to see my father standing hands on hips, his braces pushed off his shoulders, his forehead shining. 'We've been out here half an hour and you've barely begun!'

Later in the year I entered grammar school. As Bill and I were the only two in the village to make the transition my father was delighted – this was ample evidence that I was about to follow in my sister's illustrious footsteps and make good. Unfortunately his expectations were not to be fulfilled. There was a history teacher called Mr Sayers at the school whose opinions on science, creation and evolution were so far removed from Father's that I was soon told to go to the headmaster and complain. This had absolutely no effect on Mr Sayers' teaching, but a profound one on his attitude to me. When I felt ill and asked to be let out of Miss Corr's class the next week he found me alone in the corridor and knocked me flat.

If I'd had a real interest in study I might have put up with being persecuted for my father's beliefs. As I had none the main result was that I tried to distance myself from them, and got drawn into a new life with far more immediate attractions than the Brethren assembly. At first the lurid tales my classmates told of girls, liquor and cigarettes only made me feel inferior, but they held a terrible fascination, and it wasn't long before I fell in with a boy from a local farm called Joe Brown and started mitching, or playing truant. Like me, Joe loved football, and we often went to the Glenavon ground to clean the players' boots in exchange for an afternoon game. For both of us football was inspiring and exhilarating, and we played it at every opportunity, though I was careful to hide this fact from my father. What I hadn't realised then, was that competition at the assembly took account of a man's family, and that the competition had taken an unpleasant turn. Consequently word of my illicit pastime would quickly find its way into the wrong hands.

One day I came home ready to deliver a fictitious explanation of my grazed knee only to be pulled aside by my mother.

'Eric, your father's very angry.' It was a strained whisper, as though she were afraid of waking someone in the next room.

'Why?'

'You've been seen.'

'Seen? Doing what?'

'Playing football. You know how your father disapproves.'

'Who told him?'

'That doesn't matter. You're not to do it, do you hear?'

'But I want to do it. All my chums play – why not me?'

'It's wrong, Eric, and you mustn't upset your father. He's got enough to cope with as it is.'

'But –' I felt the heat of tears in my eyes. 'I don't understand. Why do you all hate it so much?'

'It's not a matter of hating it, it's just, well, it's wrong, that's all there is to it . . . ' She ran her hand through my hair, and gave a sigh. 'Oh Eric, you mustn't upset your father, not now. Do try and help.'

That evening at tea Father avoided my gaze as he usually did when I'd done something wrong, but he was also very quiet. From the few remarks he passed to my mother I gathered that all was not well at the assembly, though I couldn't understand why. When tea was over we retired to the living room. Father flicked the radio on and sat down behind a copy of the *Belfast Telegraph*, flexing the pages as he browsed. I watched him, trying for the hundredth time to fathom him out, waiting for him to put down the paper so I could read the sports page. He must have been waiting for the news, for there was a boxing commentary on the radio, and boxing was a sin just like every other sport: I'd heard visiting speakers railing against it at the assembly. Closing my eyes for a moment I tried to imagine the fight, and immediately was carried away on the surging cries of the crowd and the *biff, biff biff* of the punches that sounded like a man drubbing a leather armchair with a stick. When the pace of the blows quickened the yelling became insistent and angry, and the commentator's voice rose in pitch as though he were at the closing furlong of a flat race.

Suddenly the bell cut in. I opened my eyes abruptly in case my father had seen me listening, and was relieved to find the paper still up. With the relief there also came a vague sense that something didn't quite fit, but it wasn't until the start of the next round that I realised the pages father had been rustling and shaking smooth were now completely still. Since it wasn't like him to find any article very absorbing I kept looking at him, and a scarcely credible intuition formed in my mind. They fought the last seven rounds; a few tense seconds passed, then the referee announced a points decision.

It was then I knew I was right. I heard Father clear his throat. He laid the *Telegraph* aside, and reached for the now lukewarm cup of tea mother had placed on the sideboard beside him. He hadn't been reading at all.

The trouble at the assembly didn't stay hidden for long. By the beginning of the next year, 1949, the congregation had divided. The larger party, who for their refusal to make any concessions to worldliness were generally known as 'tight' Brethren, denounced my father and his associates as 'liberals'. (For the first time I saw clearly the significance of the piano Father had kept in the house when the gospel hall was stripped of its organ.) As one of the more literate members of the assembly, and because it was he who put up the money for the hall, my father had always held the post of correspondent, and now he was desperately resisting a proposal from the other party that this should be made a circular office. At stake was not the honour of the position but the power of the incumbent to exclude such visiting speakers as he considered doctrinally unsound. Matters came to a head at the Lord's Supper.

The custom had formerly been to give thanks and pass the bread and wine round in a large circle; but now the elements were going round twice—once for the 'tight' brethren, and once for the liberals. One day I noticed with astonishment that as soon as the 'tight' brethren had finished their communion one of them stood up and loudly gave out a hymn. The meeting nearly broke up in disorder.

This affected me badly. I'd often thought the assembly quaint, but unconsciously I had relied on it as a source of stability and truth. The folks might be eccentric, but at rock bottom, I felt, they were right. To see them squabbling with each other and betraying a code of behaviour they had up to the present almost obsessively obeyed shook me to the roots. I wanted to excuse them, but couldn't see how. And the longer the arguments went on the stronger became the uncomfortable feeling that they were guilty of hypocrisy.

It was an awkward period to be spending time with Bill's family. Bill had remained a close friend since childhood, and now I was fourteen I still spent a lot of my afternoons at the little house that opened directly on to Donacloney's William Street. His father was a relaxed, amiable man whose smile always left you with the feeling you'd missed a funny but extremely subtle joke. He was wearing it a couple of days after the fated communion service.

'Hear there was a row at the assembly,' he remarked lightly. (Nothing stayed secret in Donacloney for more than a couple of hours.)

I mumbled a reply, unwilling to be drawn.

'Funny thing, Eric,' he went on, pulling a book off the shelf, 'how Christians always say they love one another. Isn't that so? Never could figure that one out.'

He thumbed through the book, closed it neatly and held it out to me. 'By the way, this is the book I was telling you about. Darwin's *Origin of Species*. You can borrow it if you like.'

'Thank you, Mr Brien.'

'Of course you won't agree with it. You'd say God made man from a pile of dust, I suppose, wouldn't you?'

'Yes.'

'Ever think why God made us so similar to monkeys and apes?'

I shook my head.

'Well, you take a look at that, see what you think. Oh, and another thing,' he added as we were about to leave the room. 'Don't Christians believe in the Virgin Birth?'

I nodded.

'You know, that's another funny thing, isn't it, Eric? Virgins having babies. But Mary was married, wasn't she?'

I'd learned the passage by heart at the assembly. 'When as his mother Mary was espoused to Joseph, before they came together, she was found with child of the Holy Ghost,' I recited.

The smile came back to his face. 'Now tell me, Eric, if you were married, wouldn't you sleep with your wife?'

I went home at the end of that day feeling unnerved and embarrassed. I felt – quite rightly – that I was being made fun of for having views I didn't wholly understand. In the Bible studies, which were the only form of debate I was really accustomed to, scripture was decisive. I'd often heard my father rally quotations to win a point. But against Mr Brien this tactic was useless because he posed a question that was never asked at the assembly – whether the Bible itself was reliable. I resolved to ask my parents. After dinner that night Father took up his usual position in the armchair and turned on the radio. Mother was knitting. I sat down next to her on the sofa.

'I was at Bill's this afternoon.'

'And how are they all?'

'They're fine. But Mr Brien asked me a question.'

'Yes?'

I found myself lowering my voice. 'He said maybe there was no Virgin Birth. Because Mary and Joseph were married anyway, and . . .'

'Well, don't you pay any attention to him.'

'But what do I say?'

'Just don't pay any attention.'

'But – what if he's right?'

My mother became visibly agitated. There was a rustle as Father leaned forward and said tersely, 'Right about what?'

'Mr Brien said . . . he said that Jesus was probably Joseph's son, that there wasn't a Virgin Birth.'

My father glared at me coldly, then delivered the sternest warning I'd ever heard him give.

'Don't you mention that in this house again.'

It was shortly after that he was admitted to hospital for psychiatric treatment and the assembly, long divided, made a final break, the forty or so 'tight' members now meeting in the Orange Hall. This precipitated my departure. I had been feeling a gathering resentment against the assembly. For most of my childhood I'd taken its doctrines to heart: the frequent sermons on judgement and the rapture of Christian believers had more than once sent me hurrying into my parents' bedroom on a Monday morning to make sure they were still there. Now I was inclined to believe Mr Brien that Christian faith was so much mumbo-jumbo taken up like a club by ignorant men and women who in the end had shown themselves unequal to the gospel they preached. And if that was the case I certainly wasn't going to let Christianity stop me doing what I wanted to do. God or no God, I was going to be my own man from now on.

Since my father embodied all I'd come to dislike in the Christian faith he took the brunt of my rebellion. I started to affect a hard-nosed self-sufficiency, and let it be known that whether or not I passed my Junior Certificate I planned to leave school and become a policeman or a mechanic. I had every intention of carrying out the plan. When I unexpectedly passed the Certificate it was only because Father promised me a motorcycle that I agreed to stay on.

From then on our relationship found a new equilibrium, a sort of truce that allowed us to relate in day to day affairs (I later took him to work on the motorcycle), but which by mutual consent forbade any discussion of the issues that drove us apart. Seen from the outside this assertion of my will would have appeared as strength of character; but it was far from that. I was torn between my rejection of my father, and the awful, clinging urge to win his approval. Though I had stood up to him, bargained with him, even overcome him, inside I felt empty and insecure, a useless failure with nothing to show for my life but a hollow victory over someone I should have loved.

# 3: A walk on the wild side

It was a warm September afternoon and I'd taken out a couple of hours to help on a neighbouring farm with a man from a nearby cottage called Mickey Linner. Mickey would back the horse and float up to a ruck of corn then tilt the flat boards of the float to form a ramp while I slung a rope round the ruck and attached it to the winch. In this way the corn could be pulled up on to the float in one piece, and we could untie it and go on to lift the next until we had cleared the entire field. When we'd finished we collected our bikes, but instead of cycling straight home we drew up at the side of the road. Mickey produced a couple of cigarettes and we lit up. He tossed the match away.

'When did you say you'd be back?'

'No time.'

'Fancy going to the match? It's the derby.'

'Will we make it in time?'

'I reckon so.'

We exchanged smiles. In my new life Mickey Linner was part mentor, part accomplice. I'd picked up the habit of smoking at school, but often went round to his house to indulge it. We sometimes fished together. He treated me like an equal.

'How say we drop in for a drink before the game?'

'Okay.'

'Had one before?'

'A couple of sherries . . .'

'Then it's time we introduced you to the real stuff,' he said, punching me gently in the chest.

We pulled in at Livingstone's Bar in Portadown. I'd only once been in a pub before, delivering vegetables for my father. He always called them 'terrible' places, and my last visit hadn't persuaded me otherwise. Stepping into Livingstone's Bar several impressions hit you simultaneously, of warmth, of darkness, of yeasty smells and the blurred voices of men shouldering towards the bar. It looked long and seemed to open on to a street both ends until you realised that the distant windows were the ones behind you reflected in the tall, decorated mirrors. We pressed inwards where a perspiring barman was lining up glasses of black liquid. After about a dozen he stopped, scraped off the froth with a single stroke of a knife, and commenced to fill them all again. Mickey finally got his foot on the rail and asked for Guinness and a Tennants and lime.

He emerged from the press tucking his elbows in just as a boy's voice at the door announced, 'Two o'clock. No 1, Flight of Fancy; No 2, Dreadnaught; No 3, Carrie's Lass . . .'

'What was that?'

'The races. In case you've laid a bet,' he replied. 'Here.'

He shoved the pint at me. Beer spilled over my hand. 'Cheers!'

I didn't much like the taste of it, but after three rounds of Tennants I walked out of Livingstone's Bar feeling ten feet tall. Suddenly I could say anything, do anything, face anything. I could win the match single handed; I could call the other team what I liked and to the devil with the consequences; I could do so much, in fact, that I almost started three fights on the terraces by calling people names, and only Mickey's intervention kept me from getting lynched. Four hours later, and sober, I arrived back home.

No one suspected what had happened.

I had taken the first step.

Alcohol was the first of three discoveries I made around this time in my life. The second was that I could play rugby, and not only play it but play it quite well. As it was the only winter game allowed at the school I got a lot of practice and eventually became hooker for the First XV. For the away matches, of course, we sometimes had to journey by train, a freedom I took full advantage of by drinking in the licensed buffet car. More than once I was half drunk by the time I got on to the pitch. But by virtue of careful planning and the stowing of my kit inside the old organ in my room Father knew nothing about the rugby until I returned one day with a broken nose, and by then it was too late for him to stop it.

This all boosted my confidence no end, and the joy was made all the sweeter by my third discovery – that I could spin a good yarn. With a couple of drinks inside me I could spin it so well that I reduced people to hysterical laughter. Consequently, and much to my delight, I found myself in great demand whenever my rugby pals were socialising. To a teenage boy who seldom got a good word from his father this instant popularity was heaven on earth, and so I took care to cultivate my image as a breezy, successful youngster who could go the distance with the best of them. That this belied and even compensated for my true feelings concerned me not at all.

But I soon realised that my fledgling social life had to be paid for, and determined that even in the unlikely event of my passing the Senior Certificate I wasn't going to satisfy my father by following Mary into teaching—a point I made forcefully by going out to work on a farm only an hour after I'd completed my final paper in June, 1953. Though I still lived at home employment gave me a tremendous sense of power. For the first time I had an independent source of cash, which pleased me not just because it serviced my social life, but because I could contribute to my mother's housekeeping. When news arrived that I had passed the Senior Certificate and was, in the peculiar usage of the time, 'called' to Stranwillis College to begin my teacher training, I let it be known I had no intention of taking up the offer and prepared to ride out my father's anger.

Things were pretty rough at home until the autumn. Then my father approached me with the solicitous air of a man who is letting bygones be bygones.

'I've heard something that will interest you, Eric.'

I frowned at him.

'A friend of mine is leaving his job in the primary school at Seapatrick. It means they'll be looking for a temporary replacement.'

'Father, I don't want to teach. You know that.'

'You'll find it's better paid than farm work.'

That hit the mark.

'How much?' I asked casually.

'Four pounds ten a week.'

It certainly was better paid. Father pressed his advantage home. 'You don't want to be a farm labourer for the rest of your life. This way you'll be at college in a year, and well set up. Teaching has good prospects. You'll be giving yourself a future, getting a position in life. What do you say, eh?'

I'd already decided to apply, but I wasn't going to give him the satisfaction of knowing it. I turned away.

'I'll think about it.'

I was interviewed for the post not by a member of the teaching staff, but by the manager of a nearby mill that owned the school. The significance of this only occurred to me when on my first day the headmaster told me that long periods of PT displayed on the wall chart were there for the benefit of the School Inspector and not because anyone actually taught it. When it came down to brass tacks the school's function could hardly be described as educational at all; its purpose was to keep the pupil's ignorance so primed as to make a life of cheap labouring in the mill his only option. I was appalled, and told the headmaster outright that if PT was on the wall chart then the children were going to do it. He swallowed hard but said nothing. In a couple of weeks I had my class of thirty out on the football pitch and was setting up matches against neighbouring schools. Things were going so well that I even won a grudging compliment from the headmaster that I was more capable than some of the qualified teachers he'd had on his staff.

But this success was short-lived. One afternoon two boys came into my classroom in tears after getting a thrashing from the headmaster. I had in fact sent them out ten minutes before, but not for misbehaviour – only because they were a pair of troublemakers and it was easier to send them out than keep discipline while I was writing homework on the blackboard. I told them it was their own fault for going to the headmaster and sent them home.

It was in the middle of an after-school football match that an angry mother dragged one of the boys on to the pitch and, pulling down his pants to reveal an ugly six-inch weal across his buttocks, demanded to know if I'd authorised the beating. I denied it. She went straight to the headmaster, and I was summoned.

Two things became immediately apparent: first that the woman wasn't going to leave without an apology, and second that the headmaster preferred to see my copy book blotted before his own. He invited me to incriminate myself. I refused. Then I was dismissed from the room until the woman left, at which point the headmaster appeared, scowling, in the doorway.

'You,' he hissed, jabbing an upturned index finger, 'You are a despicable person. So you hope to make a career out of teaching, do you? Well you may as well forget it. And let it be understood right now that I shall not stand for any more of your insubordination –'

He never got any further, because I landed a fist in his jaw, sending him staggering back into his room. Then I picked up my briefcase and left.

I could tell as soon as word of my departure filtered through to Father. He said nothing, but for several days his face was as grim as a furnace door. Mother panicked when I told her and wanted to know what I was going to do now I'd been fired and disqualified from the dole. In fact there was no problem; I just went back to the farm until, about a month later, an advertisement appeared in the *Belfast Telegraph* for a trainee overseer in Hilden Mill. I applied and got the job, and after a sound training in all aspects of the textile industry I landed up in sole charge of a department of over a hundred women mill workers.

I soon saw that inefficiency in the mill was due to poor management. There were bonus schemes, but nobody actually received a bonus because the managers couldn't be bothered to administer it. The whole place was as slack as a worn out shoe. Not surprisingly the women in my department weren't impressed when their new teenage overseer threatened to crack the whip – they'd heard it all before, and weren't going to come back from their coffee breaks on time just to please me. So on the second day I fired eleven of them, and recruited replacements on the basis not of family connection (the usual method) but of merit. The effect was stunning. Everybody fell into line and production rose by five hundred per cent, which gratified me immensely since I'd been promised a substantial wage increase for improving output. (A side-effect of this impartial style of management was that in a predominantly Protestant town my particular department filled up with Catholics. It was nicknamed the 'Vatican'.)

During this period conditions at home took a turn for the worse. Partly the tension arose from my earning a higher wage and rubbing it in by exchanging my motor-cycle for a 1936 Ford. But the other reason was that, having more money, I was able to indulge my social life more freely. Up until this time I had been scrupulous about concealing it from my parents. Now it was more difficult.

In April, 1954, I took part in a charity match against Glenavon. Afterwards we all resorted to the Golf Club where the Armagh County team were celebrating their recent victory in the championship. The cup was passed round, filled with whisky and champagne. Joe refused to touch it, but not me: I took a draught all three times it came by, and when we left to attend the weekly rugby club dance was drunk as a lord. I tried eating some sandwiches to soak it up, but they only made me sick. I remembered little more of the evening until I woke up in the early hours sprawled across the bonnet of the Ford. Somehow I rolled home. Mother told me next day I'd climbed in through the window and lain on my bed raving and so blue in the lips she thought I was going to die. But I was up as usual in the morning, and my father, who thought I'd slept the whole night in my room, never turned a hair.

With the cheerless cooperation of my mother, who from then on regularly left a window open for me on Saturday nights, drinking and dancing with friends from the rugby club became an established routine. For all my successes at the mill it was only out drinking that made me feel really secure. I lived for it. Relations with my father were often strained, but didn't break down completely. In some ways we looked like any other father and son, except that there hung over us the constraint of subjects we could not discuss – subjects which because they touched our deepest motivations and convictions, separated us at the deepest level. About these we conspired to stay silent, yet knowing each other's thoughts made that silence scarcely more tolerable than words.

It was the summer after I first got drunk that I went to a grass track motorcycle race. A crowd of spectators had gathered on the bank outside the tightest corner; I made for it, and found myself sitting by a neat blonde. For about five minutes we studiously avoided looking at one another.

'Been here before?' I said eventually, trying to sound offhand but not too offhand.

'Once or twice.'

'Like motorcycle racing?'

'Sometimes.'

'Oh.' I let a couple of bikes buzz past. 'When do you like it?'

She faced me with a hint of a smile. 'When they fall off, of course. Don't you?'

Her name was Olive, and she came from Lurgan. I asked if she'd like to come to the rugby club dance with me, but she said her mother wouldn't let her. Sounds like my father, I said. In the end we agreed to meet for a walk by the river next Sunday afternoon, and I left the track feeling like I was walking on air.

We got to know one another quite well in the following weeks. But if I said I loved Olive it wasn't in the happy, carefree way many others fall in love. On the contrary, although we wouldn't have recognised it at the time, we were thrown together by a sense of common adversity, as though Olive's mother and my father were one and the same person. In addition Olive did work she disliked under a domineering boss, so when we got together it wasn't in the sheer joy of one another's company so much as to find companionship in our respective problems. We agreed we were misunderstood and unfairly treated, and spent long hours commiserating over it. It was not a sound basis for engagement.

Courtship didn't get in the way of my socialising. On the contrary, Olive fitted very well into my Saturday schedule. She worked till late in the shop, so by the time I'd bathed and eaten after rugby I had an hour and a half to kill before I met her, and after I'd dropped her back home at ten, as her mother required, I could get another couple of pints in before going on to the dance. Naturally Olive never knew. Deception was so familiar to me now it had become second nature.

Early the following year Mary got married. Reactions in the family varied. Mother was delighted. I liked her fiancé, Wallace, though the marriage was of little consequence to me. Father was angry and morose. Not that he disapproved of Wallace, but he had that mood about him I recalled from the months before the assembly split, of gloom in the face of a discord he resented yet could not amend. When the time came to tell him I was marrying Olive I couldn't face the confrontation and asked my mother to do it for me. Unfortunately before she had the chance, Father paid an unexpected call on Olive's uncle, who was one of his customers and had been sent an invitation to the wedding. He came home furious, demanding to know from Mother why he hadn't been told. Now the damage was irreparable; he refused to attend the ceremony – which was to be held in the Church of Ireland in Lurgan – on the grounds that as a member of the Brethren he could not enter another church. I knew I could have put things right by swallowing my pride and asking him myself, but although I badly wanted him to be there, wanted on this most important occasion to receive his approval and blessing, I couldn't bring myself to do it, and as the day drew near he became steadily more depressed and uncommunicative.

On the morning of the wedding I was folding my clothes into a suitcase in the living room when I heard the door open behind me. He came softly into the room, his eyes averted, like a child interrupting his parents' dinner party. He reached into his pocket and I felt a bundle of notes being pressed into my hand.

'Here, take this,' he said thickly.

In the one or two seconds that we could endure one another's gaze I felt as though I were looking into the bottom of his soul, to the place where his love was hidden. For that brief moment only a word stood between us – some elementary word like 'please' or 'sorry' that we could have said in spite of all that constrained us, and that would have reunited us as father and son. He would have come to the wedding, I would have been proud, and the past would have been forgotten.

But the word was left unsaid. My father crumpled into the armchair next to the radio, covered his face with his hands and wept. Feeling my own eyes moisten I turned away, stiffening every muscle against the tears. I laid the notes down on the mantel and fixed my eyes on the old chiming clock, that rigid face and the firm Roman numerals that had witnessed and measured his anger through the years, and now quietly counted through his grief.

# 4: The good life

I grew very fond of the people I met in the linen trade. Tough they might have been, but they were also kind and generous. When I got married the women I'd battled with in the 'Vatican' clubbed together and bought us a set of cutlery and cut glass.

The same could not be said of the management. All I got from them was three days off for our honeymoon in Portrush in the bleak December of 1956. Worse, my staggering increase in output wrung not a single penny more in wages. The plain fact was I worked seventy hours a week for less than a lot of the women on the shop floor. I complained about this several times without success. Finally, when I was forced to give up rugby in order to furnish our rented house, I decided I'd had enough.

The job I eventually landed was a big one, selling animal feedstuffs for Silcock's of Liverpool. It gave more or less what I'd always wanted—a company car, an expense account, and a hefty salary. It also meant moving fifty miles away to Omagh, which relieved me of the onerous duty of visiting my parents (they expected at least two visits a week) with the added benefit that my socialising—still meticulously hidden from my father—could be brought out of hiding. Olive might not know the details, but at least she had no objection to drink. At last I could dispense with the wearisome task of meeting another person's expectations.

Or so I thought. My first assignment as a Silcock's rep was a training course in London. The tutors, who used what was then a fairly sophisticated psychological method, introduced me to the idea that the rep sells *himself* before he sells his product. In other words he goes out of his way to establish trust and goodwill with the potential customer so that when a deal is in the offing that customer will come to him first. I dimly perceived in this useful little lesson that I was about to exchange a social front for a professional one. I would be wearing a different face, true, from the one I'd been forced to wear for my father, but it still wouldn't be my own. The only place I could wear that was with my friends, in the pub.

In the first few months of the new job I had plenty of chance to wear it. To start with I was living in digs; then when I found a house Olive had a difficult time with the birth of our first child, Heather, and stayed on with her parents. She and the baby had only been with me a week when both of them caught the flu, and so we were separated again. Just ten and a half months after Heather came Isobel, and another separation. Finally I was promoted, had to move to Aughnacloy on the border of the Republic, and went into digs again.

Spending so much time on my own meant the lid was taken off my social life. At the rugby club in Omagh I was among hard drinking people in a hard drinking town – even the local Church of Ireland minister seemed to spend most of his spare hours at the bar in the local hotel – so it wasn't difficult to celebrate my successes in sales and rugby with the sort of high life I'd dreamed about in my teens. I drank practically every night, and because I was young and fit I could get smashed two or three times in a week with no more ill effect than a hangover. By the time I moved to Aughnacloy and joined

Dungannon, my first senior club, I was on the crest of a wave and it was almost a disappointment to have a home to go back to at the end of the day. Socialising had become a habit I didn't want to break.

It soon became clear that Saturday mornings were tense in the house. On one of them in 1959 Olive asked me what time I was planning to get back.

'Usual time.'

' "Usual time" has been getting later and later.'

'So?'

'I just thought it might be nice for the children if you were around a bit more.'

'I'm home for dinner every night.'

'And out again straight afterwards. If it's not training, it's the pub.'

'I'm out with my friends.'

'But does it have to be every night? Couldn't you be at home sometimes? Tonight, for instance?'

I squirmed. I could have been. 'No, I can't,' I said, 'Not tonight.'

Olive got up from the table, snatched Heather's dish away and put it in the sink.

'Sometimes I wish you never played that game.'

'So what's wrong with it?'

'It's like another wife, that's what's wrong with it. Heather! Just keep *quiet*, will you? Eric, will you see to her?'

'I'm on my way out.'

'Please . . .'

She looked at me beseechingly, and suddenly straightened. 'All right, go out. I know you've important things to do. Don't worry about me doing the shopping with the children, we'll be fine . . .'

I touched her shoulder, but she shook me off.

'I'm sorry.'

'I know.'

'If I could help . . .'

'I just think you go out too often, that's all.' She turned around. 'Oh, Eric, can't you at least try?'

For a moment we stood facing one another without words, the way people do when they are about to part for a very long time. Heather observed us, and suddenly began crying again. I looked at my watch.

'I've got to go.'


If I had ever had the courage to stand back and assess the social life I prized so highly I'd have thought it very strange.

The big fella at the bar always has to prove he's the big fella. He talks loud and looks tough; he charms and dominates his circle of friends, is never slow to order another round and knows his drinks like a bookie knows his horses. But this isn't what keeps him at the top of the social pile: his real claim to fame is that he can drink longer and harder than anyone else. He can be violently sick half way through an evening and still come back for more; he can be uproariously drunk and still be wonderful company. In short, he is proud to be a drinker.

But this popularity has its price. Everyone loves the man who tells the stories and stands the drinks, but everyone hates him, too, for his ease and confidence and the attention he draws from the women. He may detect this, and it will have the effect of making him drink harder and heavier, because that is the only way he knows to keep his place, and is, he begins to feel in his blacker moments, the only thing he is really good at. Then the drinking is no longer just a social activity, but a means of proving his worth. He has to push himself that one step farther ahead to prove he's really out in front—and prove it not just to the others, but to himself.

Early in the 1960/61 season I fell badly in a tackle and broke my leg. It was a bad break with much pain; lying in hospital the next morning an unpleasant feeling came over me. I imagined it to be something like the fear an elderly person has of losing his independence and becoming an object of charity and condescension, a liability rather than an asset, someone no longer able to look after himself. Why I should have felt this way I didn't stop to think—I simply reacted to it: no one, I decided, was going to look down on me just because my leg was in plaster. If anything they were going to be astounded at how little difference it made.

By the afternoon when the entire rugby side came and gathered round my bed I'd already made Olive buy me a bottle of Scotch to hide in my locker. It was a visit the whole ward knew about, and probably helped to speed up my discharge. A few days later I was wheeled out to the car park where Olive had brought the car and eased carefully into the passenger seat by a couple of hospital orderlies, who then closed the door, waved, and vanished into the building. Olive got in the other side.

'Give me the keys,' I said.

'Why?'

'Just give me the keys.'

She handed them over under protest while I pulled myself over behind the wheel, laying my broken leg across the passenger seat and covering it with my raincoat.

'Now get in the back.'

'Eric, you can't drive, not straight out of hospital!'

'No? We'll soon see about that.'

I turned the ignition, released the handbrake by

reaching under my knee, and made a jerky start out to the road. When we had driven all fifteen miles without mishap I decided the trick was worth repeating the following week. We were due to visit Olive's parents in Lurgan. On the way back this time we were stopped by the police.

The officer leaned in through my open window. 'Know one of your rear lights isn't working?'

'Is it not? I'm sorry, officer.'

'Far to go?'

'Couple of miles. I've taken the wife and kids to see the in-laws.'

I watched his gaze pass over the empty seat next to me and prayed it was dark enough to hide the leg beneath the raincoat.

'Usually have your wife in the back, Sir?'

'Always.'

'Very sensible. Much safer. Maybe you'll get that light seen to tomorrow?'

'I will.'

He took a few paces back, and then I realised that because we were on a slope I couldn't drive away without operating the accelerator by hand. I leaned forward as though rummaging in the glove compartment and moved off with my chin on the steering wheel. I gave the officer a wave as we went by—he had pushed his hat back off his head and was gazing at me in amazement.

For the next three months, if I wasn't driving I was hobbling over to the pub on my crutches, pleased as punch when the locals said they didn't know how I did it, or that if they'd been me they'd have stayed home watching the football before traversing an icy pavement with a broken leg. But although it was a point of honour to take the injury in my stride the anxiety that arrived on that first day in hospital continued to nag me, and when I got home it pushed me over the edge. Using the toilet is always a problem when your leg's broken, but fortunately we had an outside WC with leg room and a lead cistern pipe I was confident would hold my weight when I wanted to lever myself upright. It didn't. On my first try the pipe broke and I was left sitting helplessly on the pedestal with water pouring down on my head. I sat for a while shivering; not in pain, but suddenly and powerfully reminded of the way I'd felt in Donacloney all those times I'd wanted to see a match or go to the cinema and known I could not. It was as though the intervening years of struggle and self-assertion had been momentarily stripped away and I was left impotent, and exposed. I should have done the sensible thing and called out for help: instead I burst into tears.

It was years before I grasped the significance of that day. In so far as I thought about it at the time, I identified it as the first in a line of things that started to go wrong. The second happened a year later when I arrived home one Friday to find Isobel in bed with a temperature. Olive said the doctor had already been and had reassured her the attack was a minor convulsion, not unusual for a child of Isobel's age. But when he returned at six it was to give her an injection and to send her to Dungannon hospital where she was given paraldehyde, before having a second and far worse convulsion that required her transfer to Belfast Childrens' Hospital. It was two in the morning before doctors there got her out of the fit. It left her paralysed.

By this time Olive was well into her third pregnancy, and it wasn't long after Isobel came home that she herself had to go in because of a kidney infection, and I was left to look after Isobel on my own. Fortunately the early mornings I had devoted to exercising her muscles had paid off in the easing of her paralysis, but it was clear that the fits had changed her behaviour: she now related to strangers far better than her own family, making it doubly difficult to nurse her. I decided to take the precaution of putting her in my own bed at night, as she was still suffering minor convulsions and I wasn't confident of looking after her without help from Olive. I hoped against hope that nothing serious would happen, but of course it did.

Very early in the morning I found myself pacing up and down a waiting room like a husband in a maternity unit. The difference was this was Emergency. There were no flowers, no magazines: only a barren desk behind which a nurse was reading some medical textbook, and the distant sound of doctors' voices that was worse than silence. I hoped to get word that Isobel had recovered, but when a doctor appeared it was only to say I'd have to wait another twenty-four hours for definite news. He advised me to go home. I thanked him, and he turned away, said something to the girl at the desk that made her smile, and vanished. During the slow drive back I wondered why all this was happening to me, and found myself wishing someone would come in, wave a magic wand, and make things right again. I knew no one would: there was no God, and anyway those who believed in him led lives as unhappy as anyone else's. You got what you fought for; nothing was given to you free, and if you lost it that was just too bad.

I tried to make myself some breakfast, but realised I wasn't really hungry and settled down in the living room with a book. I was too restless to concentrate. A few minutes later I was up and pacing the room, anxious, depressed and sorry for myself. As soon as the pubs opened I went in and sat alone at the bar drinking shorts, held sober by the tension like a rope pulled taut, until the time came to return to the hospital. Isobel had pulled through; I drove home in a daze, knocked back a sherry, and went out like a light.

Soon after that I was seeing a doctor myself. I explained the symptom I'd noticed writing up my accounts and he asked me to demonstrate. I held my right hand out over the table. I was trying to hold it as steady as I could, but it gave an almost imperceptible twitch. He examined me.

'Been going on very long?'

'I just noticed it.'

'You're all right apart from that? No fatigue or weakness?'

'Nothing at all.'

'Then I don't think you need worry about Parkinson's disease or MS . . .'

'What is it, then?'

He smiled. 'I understand you're a man who likes his liquor, Mr Lennon.'

'It goes with the job.'

'Then I'd say you've had too much 'Twelfth'. Far be it for me to reprimand an Irishman for his drinking, but the demon drink will occasionally . . .' He pursed his lips and smiled. '. . . take its revenge. Next time the twelfth of July comes around have a couple less, eh?'

I was relieved, but I hadn't told him about the other problem I had writing up my accounts – the problem that they didn't always add up. I recorded the cash payments made to me by my customers to tell me at the end of each week how much to bank in the company's account. The method was simple, and saved too much messing about with money during the week. Unfortunately I often found the cash remaining in my pocket was less than that due to be paid in, and so I regularly had to make up the difference from my own wages. To put it bluntly, I was running out of money.

My solution was to change jobs. I knew the agricultural sales market pretty well now, so when I was offered a job selling chickens and chicken equipment throughout Ireland and the Isle of Man I knew I was on to a good thing. The poultry industry was so disorganised that a farmer was lucky if more than fifty per cent of the chicks he bought from a supplier even survived, let alone laid. In comparison to this, a firm like mine, with a new breed of chicks that could guarantee a ninety-six per cent survival rate and a year's laying could hardly go wrong: the product virtually sold itself. And the firm was offering very attractive terms. At the age of only twenty-five I was earning, besides the now familiar car and expense account, enough money in a year to buy eight brand new family saloons.

The trouble was that far from solving my financial problems a higher salary only pushed me to wilder excesses. I'd already turned over one company car – a Morris Minor 1000 – clipping a pile of steel on my way back from a rugby match; now I started making a habit of it.

It was one of those cold clear winter days in 1961 when I was out with Jim, a second rep, delivering chicks in Moneymore. We drove two separate vans in convoy all morning at temperatures barely above freezing. By lunchtime I'd had enough. I turned in at a pub and we went for seven or eight quick ones. When we returned to the car park the afternoon had worn on, the air was noticeably colder, and we were half cut.

'You know the roads round here?'

Jim shook his head.

'I'll lead. There's probably ice about.'

'I'll be right behind you.'

'Now be careful,' I said, frowning at him. 'You stay right behind me, d'you hear?'

'Right behind you.'

'Okay.'

We climbed into the vans and rolled back on to the road. At that precise moment all recollection of Jim completely vanished. All I felt was a warm, confident sensation, as though if I drove fast enough the van would lift off the ground and fly – which in fact was what it was just about to do. I accelerated smoothly, left Jim behind, cruised a few miles then took a blind hill. Everything seemed to happen in a split second. I saw the corner. I hit the brakes. The wheels locked. I saw the hedge close on me at impossible speed then jerk down as I rode up the bank. There was a moment of near weightlessness as the vehicle took leave of the ground and a telegraph pole flew past the driver window. Then I belly-flopped into the field. Four or five trays of live chicks hit me in the back of the neck and whipped my head down on to the wheel. I thought for a second, 'Oh well – this is it,' then realised I was still alive, with blood running down my face, and travelling at a jerky twenty-five miles per hour across a frozen meadow. Seizing the wheel again I steered back to the hedge, followed it round until I found an opening on to the road, and emerged with a crazy innocent smile just as Jim appeared in the second van. The story was his party piece for months after.

But the following year a far nastier accident happened. I was giving my drinking mate Angus Watt a lift to the match at Dungannon. I'd lost the keys, so I had to start the car by shorting the fuses with a piece of silver paper. We hadn't been on time in the first place; but now we were in danger of missing the kick-off, so I stepped on the accelerator as soon as we hit the open road. We were doing ninety when I realised the truck I'd started to overtake hadn't seen me and was pulling out to pass the next vehicle in line. I jammed the horn down, but it was too late. The white retaining fence glided steadily closer on the off side, forcing us against the driver door of the truck. There was a noise like a buzz-saw on sheet metal, the snap of the retaining fence, and a dreadful roller-coaster feeling as car and truck plunged together down a twenty-foot drop. The fall lasted just long enough to create the illusion that it was going on forever, then ceased abruptly with the impact of the crash, as if we'd been put in a small tin box and dropped on concrete. We spun, skidded, and came to rest.

All of a sudden I was aware of two things: the whining of the engine and a strong smell of petrol. Angus was lying in his seat, his head tipped back, groaning loudly. His legs were trapped. I debated with myself whether I should attempt to pull him free, decided against it, and began lunging frantically at the door. It gave way. Outside the petrol fumes were even stronger. I gave myself a cursory examination to see if I'd been injured then clambered back up the bank. A woman had already stopped and was standing by the broken fence looking down. I realised my heart was racing and that I was speaking very fast.

'I've had a slight accident,' I said.

The woman glanced at the overturned lorry.

'. . . but it's all right. I want you to phone my wife, tell her I'm okay. Say I'll be home for tea. Will you do that? She'll worry, you see, if I don't get in touch . . .'

She still looked lost. For a moment I couldn't see what was wrong.

'Oh, I'm sorry . . .'

I fished in my wallet and gave her a business card.

'Eric Lennon. My wife's name is Olive.'

'You all right?' said someone else, grasping my arm.

'Yes, I'm fine. Really. If you'd just make that call . . .'

The ambulance came. There were a lot of flashing lights and policemen about. They cut Angus out of the wreckage and took him away on a stretcher. Then one of the ambulance men came over to say I should go to the hospital for a check-up. He ignored my protests, so I climbed into the ambulance with Angus. It was fortunate that I did. By the time I got to hospital I'd passed out, and was kept in intensive care for three weeks with severe concussion, thirteen broken ribs, a punctured kidney and lung damage. It was three months before I got back to work. The only reason I wasn't fired was that I was such a good salesman and the company figured a good sales record was worth a few repair bills.

I was never able to go back to playing rugby, and this had the double effect of freeing the evening I'd spent training during the week, and increasing my desire to drink. The two fitted together very well. Consequently I fell in with a couple of new drinking companions, a policeman called Jim Stonehouse and a small, sharp-witted man who introduced himself as Terry Conway. For a while everything seemed to be spinning along just as it always had: I now had a third child, Clifford; I enjoyed my social life, I was earning a lot of cash, and I still had the perfect product to sell and a horde of satisfied customers.

It was in the spring of 1963 that the chickens I was selling contracted a disease, and the telephone turned red-hot.

# 5: Directly to jail

'What's the matter with you, Eric? It's not like you to be off your food.'

I pushed the plate away. 'I'm just not hungry, that's all.'

'Pudding then?'

'No.'

'Coffee?'

'No! For goodness sake, Olive!'

'Sorry,' she said under her breath.

She began to clear the dinner table, and there was an awkward pause.

'I suppose you're going out tonight?' said Olive.

'You know I am.'

'Do you want me to come and pick you up?'

'I can get myself home.'

'I won't wait up, then.'

'Good. Don't.'

Suddenly she stopped fussing over the table and sat down.

'Eric, the children have been asking me where we're going on holiday this year. Can't we make some arrangements?'

I sighed and said in a low voice, 'We don't have the money.'

'I don't understand.'

'What is there to understand? We don't have the money for a holiday. What could be simpler than that?'

'But you earn so much.'

I looked away, annoyed.

'We don't have to go anywhere expensive.'

'Olive!'

'It's for the childrens' sake I'm asking.'

'Oh belt up, will you?'

I scowled at her, then buried my face in my fists. With things the way they were at the moment the prospect of going away for two weeks with her was more than I could bear. I didn't want to talk about it.

'What's wrong?' she said in a meek, pleading tone.

'Nothing.'

'Eric, I'm so worried about you. It wasn't like this when we got married.'

'Oh yes it was. You just didn't know.'

'It's the drink that's doing it to you, isn't it?'

'No!' I slammed my fist down on the table. 'It is *not* the *drink*!'

'Something at work?'

'No!'

'Can't we talk about it? Share it?'

'No. No, we can't. Can't you understand that?'

This time she stayed silent for a while. Then she said, 'What are Epidemic Tremors?'

I looked at her sharply. 'Why?'

'Somebody phoned about . . .'

'Oh *no*! Not another one.'

I had jerked to my feet, fumbling nervously for my house keys. 'I'm going out.'

'Aren't you going to call? I said you would.'

'No I am not going to call.'

'What do I say if he phones again?'

'Say it's the wrong number. Say I'm on holiday. Gone abroad . . .'

'I don't understand . . .'

'You don't have to.'

I went out into the hall, closing the door behind me, and leaned against the wall for a moment with a hand on my chest. I could feel my heart beating. It was irrational, like I was a kid playing hide and seek. I was actually afraid of that telephone, physically afraid of it. Having a door in front of it was no better than throwing a blanket over a grenade – I wouldn't be happy until I was away from it, out of range of that dentist's drill of a noise and that ugly little black handpiece and its angry voices.

'Mr Lennon, I've been trying to get hold of you for three days . . . Mr Lennon, I've received twenty batches from you and half of them are dead . . . It's a disgrace, Mr Lennon, and I want to know what you're going to do about it . . . I paid double the price for your product, and now . . . The plain fact is, Mr Lennon, you owe me an explanation, Mr Lennon, and I want it now. Mr Lennon? Mr Lennon!'

I dragged myself down the path and got into the car, the imaginary caller pursuing me at a distance. At least out on the road I was safe – no one could get me, provided I stayed away from a telephone. And not just my telephone. I feared *any* telephone. I couldn't stand by a public call box and not be terrified it would ring for me. And no matter how much I told myself I was panicking or tried to get a grip on my nerves, I couldn't control it. All I could do was run away, put the mask on, try and keep it hidden.

Jim and Terry had already had a couple by the time I got to the pub.

'Where's mine then?'

'Jim drank it. Thought you weren't coming.'

Jim laughed and pushed his glass across the counter.

'Isn't that true, Jim?'

'Get lost. All right, Eric, what are you having? Scotch?'

'Thanks.'

I sat down.

'So what's up?' said Terry. 'Push another truck off the road, did you?'

'If I had I wouldn't tell you so-and-sos about it.'

'How long did it take you to drive here tonight?'

'Twenty-five minutes.'

Terry swore, shaking his head. 'Twenty-five? You must have been hitting near the ton. Did you hear that, Jim?'

'On a road like that. Man, you're daft!'

'Going to book me?'

'Wouldn't bother. I'd turn you straight over to Charlie Delaney.'

'Fighting talk, eh!' Terry gave a whistle.

But Jim was smiling. 'I have to do that to keep CID in business. All CID do is sit on their butts all day and drink coffee. You know something,' Jim leaned forward and wagged a finger, 'Delaney's boss has spent so much time on the golf course since the troubles ended he's got his handicap down to two. It's a fact.'

Terry laughed. Jim took the drinks, and we clicked glasses.

'Well, Eric. Bon voyage.'

It was on my first morning back at work after the two weeks carousing with Jim and Terry that I woke up knowing something had changed. With an effort I rolled my body over and sat on the edge of the bed, rubbing my face on the palms of my hands. Olive, who had said very little over the fortnight's vacation, looked at me from the wardrobe where she was hanging clothes.

'Something wrong?'

I didn't answer.

'Just another hangover, Eric. You weren't in till the early hours.'

'I'm feeling sick.'

'Yes, I expect you are.' She primped her hair in the mirror and left. 'Your breakfast's on the table.'

One of the children must have been waiting on the landing, because Olive began to talk softly as she went down the stairs. I walked unsteadily into the bathroom, switched on the light, was dazzled, and abruptly switched it off again. I tried to brush my teeth, but my hand was shaking so badly I couldn't get the toothpaste on to the brush. Finally I slumped down on the lavatory pedestal, throwing the toothbrush and tube on the floor in frustration. My right hand twitched in my lap. I'd never felt like this before even during my worst hangovers; nausea and headaches I'd had many times, but today it was as if someone had stitched my insides through with wire and was pulling it taut, an awful raking sensation I thought you'd only get dying in a drought.

I tried to get a hold on myself. Standing up I splashed cold water over my face, wiped it crudely with the towel and returned to the bedroom to dress. Cornflakes and a glass of orange juice had been left out for me downstairs, but the thought of eating turned my stomach and I went out straight away and climbed into the car. I managed two, maybe three, calls; the customers gave me lingering glances when I dropped my pen or asked them to repeat themselves. In an hour or so I knew I was finished — I had to get to a pub. I hurried into the first one I found, threw back a couple of whiskies, and with almost unimaginable relief felt the grip in my stomach ease and the shaking subside. The cure lasted for about an hour; after that the symptoms began to come back and I was forced to return to a pub, not because I wanted a drink but because, for the first time in my life, I needed one.

By evening when I met Jim and Terry before going on to the rugby pub I was completely drunk. As usual I had a whale of a time, and, as usual, I rolled out at midnight for the short and dangerous drive home before collapsing into bed. The following morning the symptoms were there again. Once again, with the shakes and the dreadful tearing in my stomach I only managed a couple of calls before retreating to get my cure.

It gradually got worse. At night with a couple of drinks inside me I was back on top form, but during the day I felt wretchedly sick, and it was a mad scramble to get work covered in the progressively shorter periods I could last without dropping in to the next pub. A few days before Christmas I brought five bottles of whisky home to make sure I was stocked up for the holiday. Though I came home drunk every night I managed to consume the lot by Christmas Eve – when the time came to open the presents there wasn't a drop left in the house. Olive caught me looking through the empties in the drinks cupboard.

'Eric, can't you go and play with the children?'

'They've got their toys.'

'They had a father, too.'

'Leave me alone.'

'Eric, please! There's more to Christmas than booze.'

'I'll do what I damn well want.'

Suddenly she hissed at me, 'Look. I don't want the neighbours saying you're an alcoholic.'

'The neighbours can get knotted.'

'But you know how they talk.'

'I am not an alcoholic! If you're an alcoholic you're out on skid row sleeping under a cardboard box. That's what an alcoholic is.'

'Don't be so sure.'

I shut the cupboard door hard. 'Well I don't care what you think.'

'Keep your voice down. The children!'

'Will you stop telling me what to do?'

'Eric, don't.'

'That's what I hate about this place. It's all orders. Don't do this, don't do that. Well, I'll tell you, I have more fun in one evening down the pub than I've ever had here. I'm going to do what I want, and if you don't like it you can get out.'

Early in the new year I was told I could pick up a new company car, an Austin Cambridge, at Halifax. I never made it home. Swerving after I'd dozed off at the wheel I ploughed down twenty yards of fencing and landed the car on top of a tree stump. Olive had to come out and help me rock it free. It wasn't the first time I'd fallen asleep driving, so I asked Terry to act as my chauffeur and promised to pay him in booze – but it wasn't enough to stop my work running into serious trouble. For one thing the amount of time I was actually capable of seeing customers was growing shorter and shorter; but in addition to that there were times when I couldn't remember who I'd seen or collected money from. Previously good relationships turned sour, and cash ran out as expenses mounted up. By then my social life had long since ceased to be a reward for my work – it was at best a desperate search for consolation, and at worst a feeble attempt to obliterate the pains and embarrassments of the day by getting smashed at night. Olive and the family hardly figured at all. I was aware only of the clawing in my stomach, the endless backlog of calls, and the precious haven of the pub.

But worse than anything else was the fear – no longer a specific phobia of telephones or customers or creditors, but a general paranoia. It followed me relentlessly every minute of the day. Even going through my routine at the bar I was afraid the brittle facade of bonhomie I somehow still managed to affect with my drinking companions – and which was my one remaining source of self-esteem – might blow under pressure and expose me for what I knew I really was – a miserable heel.

Just after Christmas 1964 Terry came into the local to find me sitting with my head bowed over an empty glass. He breezed up in his usual way, briskly tugging his trouser legs as he sat down.

'What's up with you, then?'

'Get me a drink.'

I sensed his eyes resting on me a moment, but he ordered a double Scotch. I downed it in a single gulp.

'Hey, go easy. This isn't like you.'

'I've had it, Terry. I'm washed up.'

'That's no way to talk.'

'I mean it.'

He switched tactics. 'All right. What's the problem? Money?'

I nodded listlessly.

'How much are you out of pocket?'

'Six hundred.'

'Well, what's that? So the books don't balance. It's happened to me before now.'

I was squeezing my brow in my hand. 'Get me another.'

'Whoa, not yet. Look, Eric, six hundred's not the world.'

'It's not just money.'

'So what is it?'

He stared at me. I shifted and sighed, and he gave a knowing shake of the head. 'I might have known. Have I met her?'

'Yes.'

'Crikey, but you fellas at the club take some risks. I suppose Olive doesn't know, and now it's getting out of hand. Right?'

I nodded, and leaned back with a limp shrug. 'I don't know how it happened. Any of it.'

'You've just got to work out what you're going to do.'

'I'm leaving.'

'What?'

'I'm going to disappear. I've got almost a year's salary in payments I haven't banked yet. That should keep me going for a while.'

'Now wait a second. I've heard some stupid plans in my time . . .'

'I'm going!'

'Eric,' his voice was quiet and urgent, 'don't be a fool. Take a loan. Go to your father. Anything.'

'It wouldn't help.'

'What about Olive, the kids?'

But I was on my feet. 'I'm sorry, Terry. I've made up my mind. There's no other way.' I put a hand on his shoulder to stop him following me. 'Thanks for the drink. So long.'

I'd made my arrangements carefully. Already well-oiled and with the money in my pocket, I drove the company car straight to Dungannon station and boarded a train to Dublin. There was a hotel there I'd stayed in on a rugby tour a few years before. I booked a room, drank all evening in the bar, and then drank all the next morning. In the afternoon I went to see a film – one about a man who'd left his child. I cried all the way through it. From then on I spent almost every day alternately drinking and crying in my room.

I'd left Olive a note to say I'd be calling every day. She sounded very far away.

'Eric, is that you?'

I said yes, my voice choked.

'Are you all right?'

'Yes. I'm fine.'

'What have you done? I had the firm on the phone today wanting to know where you are.'

'Did they say anything?'

'Not much.'

I gave a sigh. Olive hesitated.

'When are you going to come back?'

'I can't.'

'I don't understand.'

'I'm in debt,' I said bluntly.

There was a silence.

'I've taken money from the firm. I can't come back.'

I called every night, growing steadily more miserable and depressed. A week into January I knew I was cornered; I couldn't stay in Dublin any longer, and couldn't go home because that would mean the end of everything. But on my next call there was a new tone in Olive's voice.

'You don't need to worry about the money.'

'What do you mean?'

'Your father can pay it for you.'

'He doesn't have that much.'

'But he can take a loan. He said you should go and square it up with the police and everything will be all right.'

It seemed too good to be true, and it was. I took the next train back to Belfast, but when I got to my parents' cottage it turned out the loan was a piece of wishful thinking. The real proposal was that I should return and throw myself on the mercy of the police. That I refused to do. I retreated to my hotel in the Republic for another few days before misery and loneliness convinced me I should get it over with and turn myself in. I decided my best chance lay in Charlie Delaney – I'd bought him enough drinks in my time, he owed me a favour. So I paid as much of the money as I had left – just over three thousand pounds – into the firm's account at the Hibernian Bank, packed my belongings, and went. The company had removed my car from the station by the time I got there, so I took a bus to Lurgan Police station.

Charlie was playing cards with a uniformed sergeant, a half empty mug of coffee on the desk beside him. He was very unlike a TV detective – a tall man dressed habitually in a fawn coloured two piece suit, with a roman nose and sharp, mistrustful eyes. With a couple of drinks inside him he had a lot of funny stories about the force; sober, he was about as communicative as a clam. He rose with a businesslike manner when he saw me, plucking a jacket off the back of his chair.

'Nice of you to drop in, Eric.'

'I think you know what it's about.'

'Let's talk.'

He led me into a bare little room where a small wooden table was illuminated from above by a light with an enamel shade.

'It's only six hundred. I paid the rest into the company's account this morning . . .'

'Let's put it in writing.'

'Do we have to?'

'It's form.'

'I realise it was a stupid thing to do – I'd like to put things straight.'

He teased a clean sheet from a folder and uncapped his biro. 'There's nothing to worry about. I just have to take a statement.'

58

I went over it painstakingly from beginning to end, stressing mitigating circumstances. Charlie glanced over the finished document. 'You went to Dublin with the intention of keeping the three thousand?'

'Yes. Is that important?'

'Could be. Read it over.'

I read it over and signed it.

'What now?'

'You'll be pleading guilty when the case comes up. That might mean a lighter sentence if we can get you into the County court rather than the Assizes.'

'You can do that?'

He cocked his head doubtfully. 'You'll have to help us.'

'I'll do whatever you want.'

'We need to inspect your bank account. Usually that requires a court order. You could speed it up by signing that you consent.'

'Anything.'

Charlie pushed me the slip of paper and a pen.

I spent the night at the police station. The sergeant only locked me up overnight, and next morning brought me a mug of tea and a plate of toast. I went to the Dungannon magistrate's court on January 14th relieved that I'd been civilly treated and confident I'd secured the best deal I could in the circumstances. I almost died to hear I was being charged with the embezzlement of the full £3700 and I was due to appear at the winter Assizes on January 28th. I could cheerfully have strangled Charlie Delaney at that moment. But protest was useless, and since no-one would sign for bail at £2000 I was led away, cursing Charlie Delaney under my breath, to be remanded in custody in Crumlin Road Jail.

Remand was hell. Remand prisoners were kept apart from the others, and because they weren't allowed to work

I spent most of my time walking in circles in the exercise yard, a fifteen foot gap in front and behind, feeling sick with desire for alcohol. The weather was dry and frosty. Along the side of the walk were toilet cubicles with half doors: you could stop if you wanted, but if you sat in one too long a 'screw' would come and look in to see what you were doing. I was sitting there when the prison PA system suddenly crackled and someone said: 'The death has been announced of the Rt Hon Sir Winston Churchill . . .' It was the end of an era in more ways than one.

After five days one of my ex-customers stood bail and I was released. I drank solidly until the trial which after the signing of the consent slip, was a formality. The charge was read, then the statment I'd made to Charlie. The Judge asked me if I had anything to say, and when I declined he gave a little speech about my having betrayed the trust of my employers and sentenced me to sixteen months. One of the sea of faces in the public gallery was Olive's; she was crying, but I hardly noticed. I felt sick, scared of prison, and yet relieved to be able to hide away. I allowed myself to be taken out of the courtroom and down some steps to a narrow corridor with lights spaced regularly along the ceiling. It went under the Crumlin Road, and when we emerged at the other end I was in jail.

I never realised it was so close.

# 6: A room without a view

I had to strip. Wallet, underpants, socks, wristwatch – everything was carefully documented and put away. There were several officers in the room; those who weren't doing anything just stood there and looked at me. Presently one of them accompanied me to the shower, then made an exhaustive search of my body, calling out distinguishing features to another, who wrote them down on a clipboard. After standing for half an hour stark naked in the presence of this group of uniformed men I was allowed to put on a brown prison uniform with a red star on the shoulder and was then put in a holding cell. Here, too, I was under constant surveillance, not for fear of my escaping but to prevent me committing suicide. The thought never crossed my mind – I felt too sick from withdrawal. The clawing in my stomach was so bad I thought my whole body would split open, and sometimes I would stand literally bashing my head against the wall to escape it. At night I suffered nightmares and woke up drenched in sweat. It was five days before there was any improvement and fourteen before I felt anything like normal.

On my first morning I was marched up to see the governor, who had a large office with fading watercolours and a view over what I supposed to be the Crumlin Road. Some distance away a figure came to an upstairs window, perhaps to see what the weather was up to or what was going on in the street. I realised neither of these made much difference to me now. There was a chair in front of the governor's desk, but he didn't invite me to sit on it.

'Lennon,' he read from a file. 'Sixteen months for embezzlement.'

'Sir.'

'We have a special wing for first offenders. They all wear that uniform. Mr Fairburn will take you to your cell at the end of this interview. I may as well say, Lennon, prison life isn't easy for any of us, prisoners or officers. In a way we're all locked up together. You'll come to see we observe certain conventions to make life easy for one another. On your side that means toeing the line and not making trouble. Live and let live. You understand that?'

'Yes, sir.'

'The other matter is your work. I see you have a grammar school education.'

'Yes, sir.'

'The informal rule is, the educated prisoners get the more responsible jobs. You know what the last prisoner did who saw me here?'

'No, sir.'

'Bank manager.' The governor allowed himself the faintest ghost of a smile. 'I put him in charge of the library.'

There was a pause while he ran his finger down a list.

'I'll put you down for the store room. You smoke?'

I hesitated, not wanting to blow my chances. 'Sometimes.'

'You can take your pay in cigarettes or snout – that's ten cigarettes or half ounce of rolling tobacco per week – or we can put two and sevenpence ha'penny away for when you get out.'

'I'll take the tobacco, sir.'

He wrote it down.

'That's all for now. You'll be allowed one visit per month to start with. For the rest, you'll learn the ropes as you go along.'

I was taken downstairs, outside, and through another set of doors to a semicircular entrance hall with red tiles that the officer called the Circle. From here the gangways of the four wings stretched away like fingers. I soon came to identify them: I'd been in C Wing on remand. A was for the grey uniformed long-termers – murderers and rapists – D for the old lags who came back in time after time. I was in B Wing, which like the rest had three levels and an iron stairway half way along. All the cells were the same – fourteen feet by seven with a bed that had to be made up army-style, a table and chair, a cupboard containing basic utensils, and a chamber pot. Mine was number 112.

The prisoner's day started at 7.30 am with the arrival of another prisoner. He was supervised by an officer and his job was to collect the slops. He didn't always find much to collect because prisoners often disposed of their faeces by wrapping them in paper and tipping them out of the six-by-four inch hole that served as a window. These 'surprise parcels' as they were commonly known were collected by yet another prisoner, also under supervison.

If it was your day of the week you might be due for a bath, but for the other six days washing had to be done using the basin and bar of soap kept in the cell. Your next visit was for breakfast. For this you were given a dixie full of glutinous porridge, a mug of sweet tea and an 'eight ouncer' – a quarter of a small plain loaf with a knob of thick marge. After that, though you might be out doing heavy manual labour, you got no more food till lunch, and then only a dixie of cold vegetables and a mug of soup. (It was a custom to dip the vegetables in the soup to warm them up.) The only other meal was tea – a piece of fruit and another eight-ouncer – after which prisoners were allowed an hour's free association to chat, bargain, play darts and cards and, as often as not, plan jobs. Lights out was at nine.

Work in the store was nothing special. The organisation was done by two officers, Mr Fenwick and Mr Crow, and if another officer came wanting something it was the prisoners' duty to go in and get it. My workmate was a cheerful young man with dancing brown eyes called Dickie Grimly. He gave me my first lesson in surviving prison life.

'What are you in for?' he asked as soon as we were out of earshot of the officers.

'Embezzlement. What about you?'

'Stole a car. Stole several; but they haven't found out about those.'

'Been here long?'

'Few months. Here, can you see if Crow's gone out?'

'I think so.'

'Follow me.'

We went up between the aisles of store goods; on our right at the top was the store office, on our left a small room with a couple of chairs and an electric ring mounted on a cardboard box. Dickie Grimly scouted around the floor until he found a dog end, then flicked the ash off it and pocketed it.

'Why did you do that?'

'What would you do if you found a fiver? This stuff's money round here. Are you working for snout?'

'What?'

'When you saw the governor. Did you take your wages in cash or snout?'

'Oh – snout.'

'Well, I'll tell you how you can earn some more. This is where the screws come for their tea break. They all come here sometime. Some of them are mean creeps, like Primble – watch out for him, but most'll let you make their tea for them, and give you a fag for it.'

I tried to take in this extraordinary piece of information, which was going to be part of my daily life from now on.

'I'll tell you something else, too,' said Dickie. 'If you can manage it, when a screw comes in for supplies, give him a bit extra. Fenwick and Crow run this place like Fort Knox, so you'll soon make a few friends. Never does any harm.'

He winked at me and grinned.

With a bit of help from Dickie I learned the ropes quite fast. When I found out one of our duties was to carry in the bread from the bakery van I asked the driver if he'd bring in some of his broken pastries as well. He obliged by delivering four trays daily, the contents of which Dickie and I sorted and wrapped in packets of six and sold to other prisoners for two roll-ups a time. With prison rations so sparse we had an excellent market. Even an officer would part with a cigarette to have pastries with his tea. In the end I built up quite a respectable trade, hiding my profits in the rafters and tubular steel bed-ends and lending it out at interest.

But although my business instincts made me a fairly rich man in the peculiar economy of the prison they almost got me into serious trouble. Dickie was right about the store officers having tight fists. If a prison department had run to the end of its budget the officer in charge was reduced to subterfuge if he wanted more supplies. Consequently when I heard that Smith, the duty officer on B2, had been chewed out by the principal officer for having rust stains on his cell walls, I knew I was on to a good thing. Not long after Smith paid me a visit.

'Any chance of getting some paint, Lennon?' He said, casually.

I pursed my lips. 'I could ask Mr Crow.'

'No – I mean any chance of getting it on the quiet.' He was almost whispering.

'Paint cans are big things to hide under your shirt.'

Smith fished in his breast pocket and produced a packet of cigarettes, sealed. In prison currency it was a tidy sum.

'Can it be done?'

I tugged out the chest on my uniform. 'Reckon I can find enough space. Tell you what. Bring me a bucket and I'll get you a bucket of washing soda. The paint'll be under the soda.'

Smith gave a nod and left. It wasn't the most orthodox sale I'd made. That afternoon I waited until we were alone in the store, then smuggled a can of paint into the tearoom while Dickie kept watch at the door. There was no need to hide it: most officers who came for tea wouldn't ask questions. But just as I'd brought it in Dickie came scuttling back to the room.

'Quick! Hide it!'

'Why?'

'Primble's coming.'

I cast around, holding the paint like a hot potato.

'Do it! Primble could blow the whole thing!'

There was a thud as Primble opened the storeroom door. In a sudden scramble I cleared the table, put down the paint can and covered it with the box, ring and kettle, turning round just in time to give Primble an ingratiating smile. He glanced at me, then glanced at the box, but didn't seem to notice it was floating half an inch above the surface of the table.

'Can I make you some tea, Mr Primble?'

'Go on. And two sugars. You only put one in last time.'

'Sir.'

I lit the ring, balanced the kettle carefully on top of it and waited dutifully with my hands behind my back. Primble blew out his cheeks. He sat dandling his cap and picking hairs off the rim. The kettle squeaked and hissed, and finally began to throw out a jet of steam. I was just about to take it off the heat when there was a sound like the discharge of a shotgun and everything under the kettle suddenly turned bright yellow. Primble let out a yell and jumped up, yellow paint all over his boots. But he soon recovered himself, and there was a knowing look in his eyes as he glared at me on the way out. Later that day I overheard him talking to Smith – he knew what Smith was up to, he said, and indicated he'd make it his business to ensure Smith didn't succeed. He never said anything to me. In fact he said nothing at all next day as he escorted me to Smith with a bucket of washing soda.

At the time I thought very little of the incident. A couple of months later I might never have undertaken it, because I found out what sort of risk I was really taking. It happened after Dickie had a visit from his wife. These visits always depressed him, and that night I heard him crying in the cell next to mine. Probably he could be heard all over the block. Finally after about two hours there came a sound of footsteps and a door opening. What happened in the five minutes that followed was barely audible, but the crying ceased, and next morning in the store Dickie was limping and had two black eyes.

After that I began to notice things. For instance, prisoners occasionally slashed their wrists to get attention, and were passed over to the prison hospital officer. In the outside world they'd have been escorted to hospital, even carried on a stretcher, but here, as often as not, they made the journey across the exercise yard in a brutal armlock, being battered until they bled. He wasn't the only one, either. A short time later it was rumoured that two escapees from the Isle of Wight prison had been brought in and had smashed up their cells in the remand block. At the time I was painting the library, which was the main reason I didn't get locked up in my cell like everyone else, and when everything went quiet I crept to the door to watch what was going on. The screws had formed a chain. I could see the two men being escorted towards me from the far end of the building. When they reached the chain they stopped and looked back, but the officers behind them simply shoved them forward. They fell into a barrage of fists, being hammered from one side to the other until they could no longer stand and had to be dragged away. On kitchen duty that evening I was sent to take them some food, so I saw the damage first-hand. It wasn't nice.

Dickie and I became good friends. He'd helped me a lot in the store, so when I got the job in the kitchen – a job with lots of perks – I got him in with me. He was shrewd, but soft-hearted. And he was a brilliant mimic, so good that with my eyes closed I really couldn't tell if the officer he was impersonating was Dickie or the man himself. A lot of the inmates in fact were real characters. Spitsy, who'd once been a boxer and was in and out all the time, was a dab hand at making alcohol. I actually saw him make it out of Brasso and boot polish. He'd been there so often that he looked on Crumlin Road as a sort of hotel and could show you sights, like the place where prisoners used to be birched. Gandry was even worse, if slightly less *compos mentis* (he used to talk to his cupboard, thinking it was a television). When he came up for release on

December 22nd he literally begged the governor to let him stay for Christmas. The governor refused. But Gandry knew the score right down to the dates of the Christmas holiday at the courts, so when he was let out at ten o'clock he simply snatched the first handbag he saw and waited to be arrested. He was in court by eleven and back in Crumlin Road for lunch.

By the end of my time I'd come to the conclusion that locking men up isn't the same as reforming them. Usually the reverse. A young first-time offender could emerge as a competent criminal. It would have been easy enough to turn to crime myself. I wasn't short of experienced advice, and once I'd got over the shock of prison life I found it tolerable, even pleasant. True the only heating in the cell was a single hot water pipe, but the jail offered a secure way of life in a society where my previous failures were if anything a source of status. It wasn't even boring. Every day brought a new battle of wits with the screws, enough to occupy your mind and keep you from regretting too long the loss of your freedom. It might seem an incongruous idea to come from a man inside, but I found myself wondering what sort of penal system it was that hardened men against the law and perpetuated criminality.

In the end I wasn't the one doing time – it was Olive, and the children. They were the ones who suffered. It was far easier to be cocooned in prison than to endure the long, lonely wait outside, aching from the past and anxious for an uncertain future. I had one big advantage: in jail there was only the present.

In early June, 1965, Dickie and I were stacking crates in the storeroom.

'You heard the news?' he said under his breath.

'What news?'

'We're getting a boxing match on Saturday. They're putting a ring up.'

'Who's fighting?'

'Jim McCourt. He's top amateur at the moment. They've put him against John Rogers.'

'I don't know him.'

'A real brawler. Should be a good fight.'

'Will we get to go?'

'Course we will. They're not going to go to all the trouble of putting a ring in Crumlin Road then stop us watching it, are they?'

'Grimly, close your mouth.' It was Fenwick.

We exchanged glances, and smiled.

On Saturday we thought of nothing else but the bout. But only minutes before it was due to begin an officer came and took me away. I wanted to know what was going on.

'You've got visitors.'

'*Now!*'

'Can't pick your moment.'

I followed him out to the visitors' building, racking my brains to think who it could be. I'd seen Olive the week before, and wasn't due to see her again for several days. Unless something had come up with her petition to the police and I was going to get out earlier than I thought. I stepped inside and sat down in front of the thick wire mesh. Framed in it like an old sepia print were my mother and father.

'Hello, Eric.'

It didn't sound like my father: the tone was too soft, too conciliatory.

'Hello,' I replied bluntly.

'How are you?'

'Okay.'

There was a pause; I shifted on the chair, uncomfortable in their presence, not sure what was in the offing.

'You've nearly half your sentence behind you now.'

'Yes. I suppose so.'

'Have you thought what you're going to do when you get out?'

'What about it?'

'Are you going to go straight?'

I sighed impatiently.

'Olive needs you, you know.'

'Yeah.'

'Will you be going back to her?'

'Maybe. Is there anything else?'

He paused. 'Your mother and I are concerned.'

'Thanks.'

I got up. There was a sob. My mother had started to cry. It happened most visits. My father said, 'Eric, please, for your mother's sake . . .'

'What?'

'Please, promise us you'll go back to Olive.'

He was pleading. It struck me because I had never heard him use that tone of voice before, never heard him beg me for anything. I had a sudden exultant sensation of power. Locked up here in Crumlin Road I had finally received a little fleeting taste of revenge for what I felt he'd done to me, and I was enjoying it. I paused a couple of seconds to take a last glance at the two shadowy figures leaning together behind the mesh.

'I'll think about it,' I said, and turned away.

It was the following Tuesday the clergyman came.

# 7: Getting back

The chiming clock on the mantel at my parents' cottage counted the seconds methodically while the family listened to mother crying.

The funeral had been torture. Making the final farewell to my father made the past draw very close, and I'd realised, looking back, that after all I'd really loved him. Death had cut through years of animosity in a single stroke. Standing at the graveside I was no longer the rebellious teenager or the heady, successful young man: I was the little boy being carried home by his father in the basket of a bicycle. Closing my eyes I'd have felt his cheek by mine and his arms around my waist as he swung me down to the ground. But he was dead, and as the coffin descended my mind was flooded with redundant expressions of love and gratitude. Now that it was too late I felt a genuine, bitter remorse.

But the funeral also had another, quite different effect on me, which no one could fully understand who hasn't been brought up in a small village. After five months in the sheltered anonymity of prison, I was suddenly thrust back into the outside world, and not just that, but into a community that had watched me depart to make my fortune and whispered at the rumours of my downfall. Their scrutiny recalled unpleasant memories.

'I'm going,' I said to Olive.

She followed me out of the door. 'Eric, please stay a bit longer. For your mother.'

'I can't stand it. They'll be watching the clock till midnight.'

'Well, stay for tea, then.'

'Olive, this whole thing is making me feel dreadful. Don't you know what it's like coming back here as a *prisoner*? They're all talking about me. Going through the village I actually heard someone say it. "There's Eric. I wonder why the prison officer isn't with him?" Do you know how that feels?'

'They don't mean any harm.'

'Not much they don't.'

'You're imagining things.'

'They probably all think I'm responsible for his dying.'

'Of course not.'

'It wasn't my fault. He was the one who drove me away.'

'Eric, you mustn't say that. Not now. Anyway your father was very kind to me after you went to prison. We owe it to him to be respectful.'

I turned away. 'Just ask someone if they'll give me a ride back to Belfast.'

She looked at me for a moment, and obeyed.


But I didn't go straight to the jail; instead I had a couple of drinks in the pub next door. The alcohol assuaged the pain and confusion as efficiently as ever and by the time eight o'clock rolled round I was cheerfully drunk.

With the funeral behind me I could set my mind on the day to day affairs of the prison. I knew if I went back at eight on the dot, the day warden would still be on duty and I'd be thoroughly searched, so I had another drink and at eight-thirty bought as much tobacco as I could stuff into two tins and headed for the gates. I was right. The night warden had arrived and I could smuggle in my full ration of snout unobserved.

That I'd been drinking pretty heavily was harder to hide, and when word got back to the deputy governor I was called for.

'Sir.'

'Sit down, Lennon,' he said. His voice was almost kind. I sat, and he went on heavily: 'It's come to my attention that you've had an alcohol problem.'

'Sir?'

It had never struck me that the alcohol was a problem in itself. Only that circumstances had driven me to it.

'Have you ever sought any help? Hospitalisation, counselling?'

'No, sir.'

'Then I think you should.'

I made no response.

'Alcoholics Anonymous holds a meeting here. I'm going to send you to the next one.'

'But I'm not an alcoholic . . .'

He fixed me with a warning look. 'Not an alcoholic, *sir*.'

The first surprise about the AA meeting was who came. I expected to be sitting in a room full of derelicts reeking of methylated spirits and wearing torn overcoats held together by string. Nobody in the room looked even remotely like they'd come off skid row, so much so that I wondered if these were all friends and relatives of alcoholics who were dead or had refused to come. They were pleasant, ordinary individuals, the sort you wouldn't have looked twice at on a bus: people like me. But when the first one stood up to speak I discovered they were more like me than I'd thought. He introduced himself by his Christian name, made a few brief remarks about his background, then talked frankly about how he'd begun

74

drinking and what, in the end, drinking had done to him. His story, give or take a few minor details, was exactly the same as mine. He too had started drinking socially, he too had neglected his family and struggled at work; he too had suffered the grasping desire for a cure, (the 'hair of the dog'), the blackouts and the fear. These experiences were not peculiar to me as an individual; they were symptoms of a disorder many people had, and that disorder was called alcoholism.

For a moment I was unnerved. But as I thought on it the connection suddenly grew remote. Yes, I had gone through those experiences, I had been an alcoholic; but, if nothing else, six months in prison had proved I could live without it. If I'd been an alcoholic before, I wasn't now. All that failure and humiliation was behind me. I was going to drink, certainly – I'd never give it up entirely – but I wasn't going to let drink get the better of me. I was going to *get back*.

Just saying it to myself refreshed me. But just how I was going to 'get back' posed a problem. Who would employ me after I'd been put away for embezzlement? The criminal underworld, possibly – for them a record was good credit. I'd already been offered five hundred pounds for information on one of my wealthy ex-customers who I knew kept large amounts of cash in the house. Even Dickie had asked if I'd be interested in buying some cheap outboard motors. Goodness only knew where he'd got them. He had them hidden in a septic tank, he said.

I brooded for a long time on my planned path back to success. But when I discovered the first step it wasn't much to my liking.

I got a visit from Olive.

'You're a bit more cheerful,' she said.

'I'm doing okay.'

I asked her about the kids.

'Heather's still having her nightmares. John's been really good with her – you know – my sister's husband, the one who teaches Sunday school.'

'Oh, yes.'

'He came round last week to take the children's photographs. You'll see them when you come out.'

There was a pause.

'Have you thought what you're going to do – when they let you out?'

I shook my head. 'I don't know.'

'Someone was asking me if you'd consider a job.'

'*Asking* you?'

'Bill Crane. He wants a salesman.'

I released my breath, leaning forward on my elbows. 'Oh.'

'It's money, Eric.'

'But with Bill . . .'

'What's the matter?'

'I just don't know if I could work with him, that's all.'

'Why not?'

'Because he's a hypocrite – like some of those people who spoke at father's assembly, preaching poverty when they're rolling in it.'

'But it's a job, Eric. That's better than being on the dole.'

I gave a sigh.

'So you'll go to an interview?'

'Yes. All right.'

'And when you come out – will you stay off the drink?'

I shook my head. 'No, I can't promise that.'

'Eric, I don't want you to get in the state you were before you came here.'

'I won't.'

'How do you know?'

'I've changed.'

Her expression through the wire mesh was doubtful.

A couple of weeks later I was granted parole for my interview and landed the job with no difficulty. Bill Crane could hardly be charged with altruism – he was getting a good salesman dirt cheap, and he knew it. There followed another ten weeks of internment, but now it was hard to settle down again, and I was glad when the governor decided to shorten my sentence by giving me Christmas parole. Glad, that was, until the day came and I faced the prospect of returning to my old haunts with a new reputation.

Olive met me at Crumlin Road on a crisp winter morning three days before Christmas and we took the bus to the station. There was no car now.

'The kids are really excited,' she said.

I managed a smile. 'Will mother be there?'

'Yes. She came to look after them while I met you. She's done that lots of times.'

'It's not going to be much of a Christmas, is it? I mean they've been used to lots of presents . . .'

'I've managed to save a bit.'

'On social security?'

'Sixty pounds.'

'I don't believe you.'

She produced twelve five pound notes from her purse, and handed them over.

'Shall we do some shopping before we get on the train?'

'You bet we will.' I smiled at her. 'Hey, there's just one thing. Something I've got to pick up.'

'Please, Eric. Not the pub again.'

'I'm not going to drink. Promise. I'll be right back out.'

I was collecting a Christmas present—a gold watch a prisoner had sold me for two ounces of snout. Once I was inside the pub I thought it couldn't do any harm to have a quick one for lunch, so I stayed for an extra ten minutes, and then I got talking and had another one, and another, and finally rolled out at four, completely drunk. At home the children greeted me affectionately—they were used to my drinking now. Mother cried.

But I had no physiological addiction, and beginning with Christmas—which turned out to be the best we'd had for years—I threw my energy into 'getting back' and stayed off the drink. For the three months I was working for Bill Crane I had no time for socialising anyway. It was a slow moving business and getting orders was hard work even when I had a reasonable product to sell. When the firm lost an important contract on the supply side it got even harder—like playing rugby with two men sent off—and I felt pleased with myself when I finally clinched a deal. Crane, though, was unimpressed when I raced into the office to tell him. The reason was simple—he already knew, because he'd got the order himself. He would have saved himself trouble by declining to point this out, but he did so, and when I argued about it he added with a gesture at his partner in the next room that in hiring me they'd seen themselves as charitably helping a lame dog over a stile. I replied that I didn't see twelve pounds a week as charity, told him what sort of Christian he was, and walked out.

'Getting back' on my own wasn't easy. First I borrowed three hundred pounds off my mother to start a vegetable round. It flourished for a while, but then I started taking what I called 'breakfast' in a place called the Baker's Club that opened at four in the morning to serve the night-shift workers. Gradually I spent more time drinking than delivering vegetables and the business flopped. I got a job on a coal lorry, but the combined effect of heavy labour and a dreadful spell of weather forced me to quit, and instead I started driving a tipper lorry on a motorway site. It wasn't much better: dumping fourteen tons of rock one night the hydraulic arm gave way and shot through the cab window, missing my head by inches. I finished up having to lie on my back and kick the rocks on to the road.

In the middle of summer 1966 I took myself in hand and thought hard about what I was doing. Jobs like these weren't bringing in enough money to look after my family, let alone socialise, and we had another child on the way. On top of that they were very hard work. So why wasn't I going for something better? Was I too ashamed to face selection? There seemed to be only one answer – swallow my pride and go for a decent job.

My first interview was with a Mr Hamilton, for the post of transport manager in a firm making galvanised water tanks and garbage cans. He came straight to the point.

'Well, Mr Lennon, I can only say that you're over-qualified for a position like this. Why do you want it?'

I took a deep breath and laid my cards on the table. I'd been an alcoholic, I said. I'd got into debt, embezzled a large sum of money from my employer and done a year in jail. I had no money. I wanted a break. Did he want to go on with the interview? To my great surprise he did, and I was hired as transport manager at about the same wage Bill Crane had offered me when I came out of prison. I was delighted. At last I'd got my foot on the ladder.

The climb was unexpectedly fast. Soon after I joined, the company hit a financial crisis. But although the managing director was at his wits' end I knew from my own business experience that the firm was a viable concern, and had only run into trouble because it was top-heavy with overheads. I suggested a rescue plan to him that reduced overheads by forty per cent without affecting workforce or production, and extended my responsibility from transport into sales. He went for it, and after twelve months of hard work streamlining the company and attracting new customers, sales went up by over a hundred per cent. My salary and reputation leapt up in proportion. All of a sudden I was earning again; so much so that by 1969 I'd managed to put away a thousand pounds.

My break came the same year. No sooner was the firm back on its feet than the director entered a price fixing ring with his competitors, with the result that prices were jacked up by half in a matter of months. There was no inflation and no rise in the cost of materials – the profits went straight into the owners' pockets. I saw my opportunity and took it. With the money I'd saved I bought a diesel welder, a spray plant and an old banger of a lorry, hired a couple of men, and started up a light engineering firm in my own back yard. Running the thing on a shoestring kept my prices so low it was the simplest sales job I'd ever had to go around the customers I'd won for the other company and invite them to buy from me instead. In one year the turnover rose to a quarter of a million, the staff increased to twenty, and we twice had to move to larger premises to accommodate the extra demand. It was a real family business; the kids helped out in the factory, and if I had little spare time in the early days (I often got up at seven and didn't get to bed till two) that was more than made up for by the satisfaction of building my own business and taking the custom away from my old firm while I was doing it.

It was this sense of success that steeled me to take up my social life again. This time, however, it was going to be far more carefully managed. I was after more than pleasure;

I wanted respectability, and to get that I was prepared even to go to church. Consequently most Sundays I took the whole family along to the High Street Presbyterian Church in Lurgan. I'd first been introduced to it by Mr Hamilton, and soon got on friendly terms with the minister, an ex-misssionary called David Mckee. Not that I allowed this to interrupt my more familiar social habits. By 1971, with business booming, I was back in a social circle – this time at Glenavon soccer club – and acting as chairman for a local junior side that went on to win five trophies. I was riding the crest of the wave, unaware that it was just about to break.

# 8: The man in the glass

I had a customer who'd given me a contract to supply three tanks to a hospital in Londonderry then defaulted on his payment for the third tank. Knowing Johnnie Airdrie had a drink problem I decided I'd invite him out to lunch, buy him a couple more rounds than he could take, and get him to write me a cheque when he was too blocked to know what he was doing.

It took longer than I'd anticipated. At half past six he staggered out of the pub and headed for his car.

'Well, I've had a great day,' he declared.

'It'd be a better day if you gave me that cheque for twelve hundred pounds.'

He patted the breasts of his jacket rather too ostentatiously and shook his head. 'Didn't bring the blasted thing with me.'

'Johnnie,' I said through my teeth, 'I want that cash.'

That sobered him a little.

'Okay,' he said, unlocking the driver door, 'Come back for a last round, and you'll get it.'

I looked at my watch. I'd agreed to take Clifford out to Portadown for a trumpet lesson at seven. On the other hand I was determined to get my hands on the cheque, and if that meant going back with Johnnie then so be it. I followed him home.

'There you go,' he said, filling two glasses unsteadily.

'You've only got gin?'

'That's it. And no money till you drink it.'

Gin was one spirit I'd always loathed, but I threw it back.

'Now what about the cheque?'

'Sorry,' said Johnnie, sitting down heavily on the sofa, 'I never write cheques when I'm drunk.'

I stalked out in a furious temper, phoned Olive from a call box to say I'd been held up, and practically flew home to collect Clifford. The sun was very low, but it was only when I came over a hilltop at sixty and was completely blinded that I knew I was in trouble. The lamppost flashed out of nowhere to smash into the left headlight and send me spinning over, brakes full on. Next thing I knew I was being hauled out of the wreck by a couple of policemen. My only reward for the afternoon's work was the loss of my driving licence for a year.

For this considerable inconvenience I laid the blame fairly and squarely on Johnnie Airdrie's shoulders, and compensated by drinking longer on my thrice weekly visits to the Glenavon club. It was a comfortable routine I easily slipped back to, being the big fella, the life and soul of the party, the person who is always ready with a joke and is always right. After being robbed of my licence being right was so important to me that I was willing to set up ridiculous contests to prove it. When a friend called Billy Wilson boasted how much tonic wine he could drink I stood him a bottle – enough for four or five men in a night – bet him a fiver he couldn't down it in half an hour. He managed well enough at first – half the bottle had gone in fifteen minutes. But he got steadily slower, and finally collapsed just before the half hour was up.

But at thirty-six my body wasn't standing up to alcohol as well as it used to, either. One Sunday morning I woke up feeling like I'd got diarrhoea and found I was haemorrhaging from the liver. The doctor sent me straight to hospital, where I was strung up and bled until midnight. The story must have got around because later on I got a visit from George Averly, an elder at Lurgan church. He got a tongue-lashing before he left. As being 'right' covered my social habits in general I wasn't in the mood to have them moralised over, even if I was a bit the worse for wear.

The licence was restored just in time for me to go to the Ballymena Show. On the day before I'd intended to make some calls in my best sales area, Coleraine, but arrived to find the town cordoned off. The troubles had flared up again, and six people had been killed by a bomb planted in an off-licence. Consequently on the day of the show I had to get two days' work done in one. I left home at seven-thirty on one slice of toast, made it to Coleraine by nine to do my calls, and finally emerged from the show at six with a customer in the pasenger seat. I would have headed straight home if the customer hadn't seen a policeman he knew on duty at the gate and invited us both for a drink. The next two hours were spent with a group of policemen and policewomen in a nearby pub. Eight rounds later I got into my car only to be hauled in by a police reservist.

I followed him into the station, fists clenched in my pockets.

'Wait here.'

He disappeared into a side room to fetch a doctor. A blood sample would be taken. If it was over the limit – and it almost certainly was – I was in trouble. I glanced round the room. Just then a couple of the policemen I'd been drinking with came in. You can get to know people quickly in a bar, and they seemed like old friends. I felt relieved, as if I'd found an ally, and raised a hand.

'Afternoon.'

They ignored me.

I cleared my throat loudly. At that one of them glanced in my direction, but there was no hint of recognition in his eyes. I might have been a stranger walked in off the street. I might even – and here the grim possibility dawned on me – have been set up. I felt a momentary surge of anger, but there was no escape. After all I had been driving the car when I was stopped, if only in the car park.

'Mr Lennon, would you come this way, please?'

In the two weeks between receiving my summons and attending the court hearing I drank heavily almost every night. I was bitter at being caught so soon after I'd got my licence back, and doubly bitter that I'd been led into a trap. Of course I couldn't prove it, and it would have done me no good if I had. But I detected a hint of the old paranoia returning, the feeling that there were people out there determined to get me.

'They've taken it away for five years,' I said to Olive, coming home after the trial.

She gave a little sigh.

'It was a set-up. I *knew* it was a set-up.'

'There's nothing you can do.'

'If I could get my hands on those . . .' I shook my fist and brought it down on the counter. 'I'd wring their necks.'

'There's nothing you can do,' she repeated.

I began to pace the kitchen. 'How am I supposed to run a business when I can't drive?'

'We've managed before.'

'Barely.' I clicked my tongue. 'Five years. *Five years!*'

'I'm sure if we sat down to think about it . . .'

'Why bother?'

'We can find a way.'

'It's not going to work out, can't you see that? Somebody's got it in for me.'

'Of course they haven't.'

I fumbled the car keys out of my pocket.

'I'm going to the club.'

'Oh Eric, not again.'

'Yes. Again. It's about the only place I get any sympathy.'

'Then let me drive you.'

'I'll drive myself.'

'Eric, if you're caught again it's an automatic sentence.'

'Watch me.'

I stalked out and began a two week binge that ended in my being taken to hospital. For seventy-two hours they dried me out using parentrovite injections and pints of water to sweat out the toxemia and replace the body fluids I was losing through the dehydration of alcohol. Then they put me on antibuse treatment. I was given antibuse tablets then told to drink a single measure of vodka. That will normally produce a sudden drop in blood pressure followed by drastic swelling in the head and neck, a reaction severe enough to deter the patient from taking another drink. In my case the first vodka had no effect at all. They gave me a second, then a third. They weren't permitted to give me any more, so I was returned to my room in the company of a male nurse, who took the rest of the bottle of vodka in his pocket. I attacked him in the elevator, but he fought me off, which was fortunate because if the reaction I got eight hours later had been any worse it would have killed me. For all that, antibuse failed to deter me. When I got home I just flushed my supply of tablets down the lavatory. The fact was I wanted to drink. I wanted it so much that when I found my friends at the club drank too slow I arranged with the manageress to pick up an extra double Scotch every time I went to the loo. I wanted it so much that when Olive got fed up with driving me to the club every night I moved house so I could walk there.

One morning I woke up lying on the sofa with a blanket over me. Olive was drawing back the curtains.

'It's half past seven, Eric.'

'What?'

'Half past seven. The kids'll be down any minute. Get up.'

She pulled the blanket off.

'Look at the state of you. You'll have to get changed before you go to work.'

'I can't face it . . .'

'Yes you can.'

I shook my head.

'Eric, you're the centre of that firm. It needs you.'

'It'll get along without me for a day.'

'You missed work yesterday. That's already five or six calls overdue.'

I knew she was right, and motioned with a hand. 'All right, all right, I'm going.'

Olive left the room and I heard Clifford's voice in the kitchen. I couldn't remember a thing about the night before: I must have had a skinful because I could see the telltale white blisters of alcohol on the back of my hand. I rolled myself upright and sat for a minute or two, head pitched forward. Not only did I feel too ill to go to work – I had no desire to go. It was simpler to quell the feeling of unease by putting off uncollected accounts than by going out and doing them. On the other hand the fear of having the firm suffer registered more powerfully in my mind than the fear of going to the factory, and I finally forced myself to get up.

In the five hours I spent studying the firm's accounts I managed about half an hour's real work. Though I promised myself I'd stay at it till four the clawing in my stomach was so unbearable by three-thirty that I phoned Olive to take me home, and retreated thankfully to the club, exhausted with the effort of trying to overcome my fears and content instead to drown them. The next day the same thing happened; the day after that I stayed at home. So it went on – a couple of days working, a couple of days not, until I was going through the motions of normal life without accomplishing anything.

'Eric, you have *got* to go in. The firm will slide without you.'

'It's all right,' I said with a dismissive wave.

'How long have you been drinking?'

'I've been at it all day.'

'We've just lost another order.'

'So what?'

'So you're going to sit by and let your efforts go to waste?'

I turned on her angrily. 'Well? What do you expect me to do? How can I see customers when I can't drive?'

'That's not the problem.'

'It's not my fault we've lost that order. I can't help it if the police victimise me. Go and blame them.'

'I wish you'd stop feeling sorry for yourself.'

'You'd do the same.'

'You know perfectly well you could get those orders if you wanted to.'

'You're not the one who's lost a licence, are you?'

'Well that doesn't mean you have to make it worse by getting drunk every night, does it?'

'Leave my drinking out of this.'

'Your drinking is the problem.'

'Yeah, yeah.'

'You know it is.'

'Oh get knotted, Olive!'

I was slumped in an armchair by the hearth, Olive was perched uneasily at the dining room table. The little posy of flowers someone had put in the centre of it had wilted, leaving a halo of dried petals on the polished wood.

'Where are the kids?'

'At church.'

'At church? It's Wednesday, for heaven's sake.'

'There's a youth club. Clifford goes to Boys' Brigade, remember?'

I gave a grunt. 'What is this youth club?'

'Just something for young people at the church.'

'You shouldn't let them go.'

'I encourage them to go.'

'To a church?'

'Why shouldn't I?'

'Why *should* you?'

She stood up. 'If you really want to know it's so they don't have as much chance to see you rolling drunk.'

'They don't notice.'

'And when was the last time you even talked to them? Geoffrey's seven and he hardly knows you.'

'That's not true.'

All of a sudden I felt afraid as well as angry, and pulled myself up.

'Where are you going?'

'Where do you think I'm going?'

'So when shall I come out to bring you home?'

'Very funny, Olive. I'm sure my friends will help if I need it.'

'That's what you think.'

'And what do you mean by that?'

'That they're getting fed up with it. Used to be three or four of them brought you back. Now it's one. He just leaves you on the doorstep and rings the bell. Carry on like this, Eric, and you won't have any friends left.'

I dragged my tie off and threw it down as I left the room. 'Well it won't be the first time, will it?'

Without sales promotion and fresh orders the business slowly began to lose ground, but the fear of liquidation no longer galvanised me – it just made me drink. I was past the stage of wanting solutions. I had the solutions – it was excuses I was after now. If my plans were going to fail it mattered only that the failure shouldn't be my fault. I'd blamed the police. Now I needed another scapegoat.

At first I didn't recognise it. News emerged that a UDA man had been shot by the IRA on his way to work. A reprisal was organised, and two men went out with the intention of shooting a Catholic. When they couldn't find one they got drunk and holed out in the grounds of a chapel on the edge of the Ardoyne, a Catholic area of Belfast. In the early afternoon they saw a man approaching them on the Protestant side of the street. They didn't recognise him, and when he crossed over near the chapel they assumed he was a Catholic and opened fire. Olive's brother-in-law, the one who had taken the photographs and looked after the children when I was in prison, died instantly. He had been crossing to collect a prescription for his seven year old daughter.

Initially I was shocked. Then I felt angry at the IRA for the reprisal that led to John's death. But by the time the funeral was over I almost felt relieved: now I could indulge my drinking for a perfectly respectable reason. A week later I hadn't been to the factory once, and I'd spent more time at the club than most people spend at work. I had what I wanted, and it was sheer, unadulterated hell.

No two alcoholics experience their hell in exactly the same way. I'll try to tell you about mine.

Every day was the same. I crawled out of bed, went downstairs and threw a handful of librium or distalgesics into my mouth. I'd still be drunk from the night before, but still craving alcohol and feeling sick as a dog. If I could face going to work I'd have a warm bath to revive myself, then measure out the rest of the day in Scotch. If not, I'd just lie in bed drinking jug after jug of orange juice to fight the dehydration. Either way I'd be back at the bar by opening time, shaking like a leaf, needing two or three quick ones to get me steady. I'd be first in and last to go, and if I was still sober enough to stand by the end of the evening I'd take a carry-out to keep me going into the early hours. Finally, alone in the house, I'd crawl into bed or sink into the oblivion of sleep on the floor.

Whole stretches of time would vanish from my memory. Quite often I'd talk to someone for two hours and next night, when he asked me about something I'd said, would have forgotten every word. I'd have to improvise, make things up. Still I played the big fella, bought the rounds, made the most noise. But I never knew if anyone really liked me. I was perpetually lonely and gripped by a horrible, rootless fear. I suffered hallucinations. I couldn't eat. I wanted to throw up but could only dry heave. All the time my stomach had the clenched, raw sensation of being raked over with blunt knives. I wanted to live, but sometimes wished I was dead.

I knew sooner or later I was going to hit the wall. It was only a matter of time before I got into debt and did something stupid that would land me back in jail. Already I was dodging my creditors. Olive was doing some of the collections, but I hardly ever saw her, and if she tried to talk to me we ended up having a row. Small signs told me the children still occupied the house – shoes on the doormat and dishes in the sink – but I seldom saw them. My life was reduced to a routine as severe as that of a labour camp. It was existence under compulsion.

After eighteen months of addictive drinking I was propped against the living room windows when Clifford walked in. Seeing me he would usually have turned on his heel and crept out again, but he came forward, offering me an exercise book. I knew what it was.

'So this is your essay?'

'I got it back today.'

'Did you get a good mark?'

'Ten out of ten.'

'Good for you.'

I flipped open the first page and read a couple of sentences at random:

It is improbable that any person ever set out to be an alcoholic. It is a gradual process which takes place without the victim realising it.

There was a large red tick in the margin by that. Flipping through the rest of it I saw it was full of ticks. At the end Clifford had concluded:

If a person is in doubt as to whether he is an alcoholic or not he should answer the twenty questions listed on the next page. In order to keep him honest he should also read *The Man in the Glass*.

The twenty questions came on an AA tract I'd seen years before in Crumlin Road; *The Man in the Glass* was a poem. I turned over the last page and found a second poem. At the top Clifford had written:

Many songs have been written about alcoholism. I think
that the most tragic is as follows.

It began:
My father is a drunkard, my mother she is dead;
And I am just an orphan child, no place to lay my head.
All through this world I've wandered, they drove me
   from their door;
Someday I'll find a welcome, on Heaven's golden shore.

Up to that point I had been reading an essay written by
a schoolboy. But suddenly nausea overwhelmed me and I
wanted to burst into tears. Clifford wasn't writing about
alcoholism at all – he was writing about him, and me. My
eyes roved the page as I struggled to fight his pain, and
fixed on the red scrawl underneath. It said three-out-of-
ten. I said aggressively, 'I thought you got ten out of ten.'

'That was for the content and presentation.'

'Why did the teacher mark you down to three?'

'He said . . .'

'Yes?'

'He said I missed something out,' Clifford blurted.
'That alcoholics can be healed if they accept God and
believe his promises.'

'And what the blazes does your teacher know about
alcoholics?' I demanded.

Clifford said nothing.

'Torture. That's what being an alcoholic is about. I'm
being tortured. God can't change that.'

I shoved the book back into his hand, and swallowed.

'Here. Well done. And you can tell your teacher from
me that he's got as much sense as a cabbage.'

Clifford retreated and I turned back to the window. It was a calm, sunny afternoon. A beach and park afternoon. Passing high overhead were ragged lines of geese flying south. Next door my neighbour, a reserve policeman, glanced at the sky as he locked his car and walked up his garden path. A child ran out to greet him, and he swung her up in his arms. The closing of the front door sent a slight shudder through the room. Slowly I raised both my hands and placed them on the glass, applying a slight pressure so that from outside it would have looked as though I was trying to push a window open. It was firm.

After a few minutes I trudged upstairs to get ready for a visit to the club. My anger had evaporated and left a residue of fatigue and melancholy. I made my way to the bathroom, meaning to wash my face; but after I'd filled the sink I laid down the soap and stared into the mirror. The man in the glass was looking at me with a sort of sneer.

'My father is a drunkard,' he said. Then, 'That about sums you up, doesn't it, eh, Eric?'

I glanced down into the clear warm water, and back up. Our eyes met.

'Let's face it. They'd be better off without you. I mean you're not exactly the ideal husband and father. You hardly even belong here any more. If it weren't that you bring in an income . . .' He shrugged casually but almost spat the words out: 'you'd be completely useless.'

I looked away; but I didn't leave – now that I'd begun I wanted to say it all, no matter how much it hurt. When I faced the mirror again the man's eyes were trained on mine.

'Let's look at the facts, Eric. Number one, Olive and the kids managed perfectly well without you when you went into Crumlin Road. True? *True?*'

I nodded, and he nodded with me.

'Number two. In a matter of months your business – the only thing you ever did for your family – is going to collapse, and when that happens you will be a dead weight, a liability. Number three . . .'

I took a deep breath.

'Number three, you're insured for ten thousand pounds. Enough to pay for your children's education.'

'And Olive?' I said, momentarily closing my eyes.

'Olive would be happier with you gone. Don't you think,' he said, raising his eyebrows slightly, 'that you'd better do the decent thing . . . ?'

The man in the glass stared at me, not blinking. The eyes were dead and resigned, too creased at the corners, as though he'd spent his life gazing against the sun. He looked older than his forty years.

We dipped our hands in the water and let it trickle through.

'The decent thing,' we said together.

# 9: Doing the decent thing

It was the sort of splendid summer afternoon when the sun's brilliance makes the coutryside look dim and dry. The shadows had retreated beneath the hedgerows. The road was dusty, the windscreen of the mini smudged with flying ants. There wasn't another car within a mile of us, and that conferred on the place a delicious secrecy I recalled from my childhood, when you were away from the houses on your own and no one could spy on you.

'Are you all right?' said Olive, glancing at me.

'Why?'

'It's not like you to want a drive in the country.'

'I just thought it would be nice.'

She said nothing for a couple of minutes.

'You haven't been drinking these last two days.'

'You're not pleased?'

'I can't believe it's going to last.'

'It's just my ulcer bleeding again.' I made myself smile. 'You still like motorcycle racing?'

'Sorry?'

'Do you like motorcycle racing? I said that to you when we first met.'

'What did I say?'

' "Sometimes." '

'Well, I suppose I still like it, yes.'

'Perhaps we should go again some time.'

'Eric, what's up with you?'

'I'm asking you out on a date. Going to turn me down?'

'I don't understand you sometimes.'

A signpost appeared in the distance. I'd been counting the turnings off the Dromore Road since we left Lurgan: this was the fourth. I stretched my hands down between my knees.

'I think I'll take a walk. Do you want to drop me off at the crossroads?'

'Why here?'

'If I start here you can meet me in Waringstown. McCabe's pub.'

Olive looked doubtful.

'Are you sure you'll be okay?'

'What's going to happen to me? You think I'm going to get struck by lightning?'

'How long shall I give you?'

I glanced at my watch. 'Couple of hours.'

She slowed down. I climbed out of the mini and stood by the signpost to Waringstown.

'Two hours, then.'

'McCabe's. Thanks, love,' I said as she pulled the door closed, and bit my lip.

The mini moved away with the characteristic deep puttering sound of a car with a failing exhaust, and the woman I'd lived with for twenty years vanished into the haze. I was alone with the heat and the insects.

I'd never had the least intention of walking to Waringstown, nor, badly as I craved a drink, would I be waiting in McCabe's pub. Instead I struck out in the opposite direction towards the little derelict cottage that had once been my home, and the river. There was a tingling lightness in my stomach like a singing of crickets, but that was all: the rest was silence and resolution. I'd lied about my ulcer – I had one all right, but I'd laid off the drink so people would know when they found me that this had been a balanced decision and not just an accident – it took the place of the suicide note I couldn't leave for fear it would be found too soon. I didn't want to be discovered now any more than I'd wanted to face the outside world when I was in prison, and I'd taken careful precautions to ensure that my death – like my rugby and my drinking and my failure – would stay hidden for as long as possible. Olive would turn up at McCabe's at half past two, spend maybe thirty minutes asking for me, call the police, then go home to wait, quietly, as she'd always done. I'd probably be found the following morning.

I was on a familiar route. It led to one of the deep pools in the river not far from the old cottage, where I used to bathe after a day on the farm. To get there I had to cover about three miles to an old stone bridge by a factory that made plastic pipes. Once over the bridge I could get off the road and follow the riverbank. I'd already made up my mind there'd be no stopping. I'd march straight into the pool. 'I'm going to do it, I'm going to do it,' I said under my breath, walking rapidly, my eyes fixed straight ahead. At the bridge the road turned sharp right; I followed it, aware of the dark water creeping past underneath. The pool was in sight now. 'I'm going to do it, I'm going to do it,' I breathed, and suddenly I could hear the sound of the river, a delicate rippling, and in the distance a noise of tumbling through shallows, relentless and insistent, like a car being driven at high speed.

Olive had gone straight to my mother's. When Father died she had stayed in the cottage for a little while, then moved in with us, then, because of my drinking, moved a third time to a house of her own. She asked Olive in, but they talked in the hallway. Olive had a nagging feeling that I wasn't meaning to go to Waringstown.

'Why didn't you ask him?'

'I was afraid he'd get violent.'

'Where would he be going?'

'How far is it from that crossroads to your old cottage?'

'Three miles. Why?'

'He's been talking about the past a lot recently. Sometimes in the middle of the night he rambles about things that happened in his childhood.'

'But why would he deceive you?'

They looked at each other, and read each other's thoughts.

'What are we going to do?'

'I don't know.'

'Shouldn't I go after him?'

'Are you sure he didn't go to McCabe's?'

'I suppose I could phone . . .'

But there was no one by the name of Eric Lennon at McCabe's. Olive tried the doctor. He said if she suspected a suicide she should go out and start searching. He would make arrangements for a place in the local psychiatric hospital. At that she flew out of the door, and soon arrived back at the crossroads. There was nobody there. She got out of the car, looked down the road towards Waringstown, and seeing nothing set off towards the old cottage, praying as she'd not done for years. It was approaching the bridge that she saw in the distance a small figure. She closed in, and had mounted the bridge before it turned round, froze, then made a limping dash for the bushes on the verge. Suddenly she was past, skidded to a stop and jumped out.

'I know what you're going to do!' she cried.

'Mind your own business,' I said. But I was faltering – this was an Olive I'd never met before.

'I'll do no such thing.'

'Olive, please, you know I'm no use to you. I'm just doing what's honourable . . .'

'Oh, *honourable* is it? Abandoning your family is *honourable?*'

'There's the insurance.'

At that her face turned white with anger. 'Those children don't want money. They want a father. Taking that away from them isn't honourable. It's cowardice.'

'Let me go. I'm going to do it.'

'All right, Eric. But let me warn you. If you go in that river I'll go right in after you, and then the children will have nobody.'

I sagged. Suddenly I found myself thinking of Heather, of the nightmares that had woken her screaming at night when I was in prison, and then of John, and the little girl who now had no father. Olive had circled round, and was backing me towards the mini.

'Get in.'

I wondered if I should fight her, try to run away.

'I said, *get in!*'

Next moment I was sitting limply in the passenger seat with the hedgerows flying past on either side. Olive took me straight to the psychiatric hospital, where I stayed conscious long enough to tell the ward sister to keep clergymen away, then fell into a deep sleep that lasted for almost forty-eight hours. There were three agonising days of withdrawal before the shakes set in, then a long, gradual recovery. The doctors consulted over an appropriate treatment. Antibuse tablets had failed the first time round, so they decided on electro-convulsive therapy. No reason was given. They just wheeled me into the treatment room on Friday morning, performed the ECT, and let me go home for the weekend as soon as I'd recovered. By Friday night I was drunk and stayed that way all weekend. After that they kept me in except for special events, like an outing to the Ideal Home exhibition at the King's Hall, and even there patients were kept a close eye on. (Not that this stopped me drinking. They'd supervised all the public bars but forgotten about the members' bar, so I got successfully stoned.) Eventually I was transferred to a private ward where I was fretful and solitary, but dry. Three friends from the club brought me fruit, but it wasn't the same as when I broke my leg playing rugby for Dungannon. They were stiff and subdued, and left after ten minutes. I never saw them again.

Olive on the other hand visited as often as she could, and turned up one day with a couple of blue account books under her arm. She gave me a kiss and sat down beside me on the bed.

'How are you today?'

'Okay.'

'I've had a word with the doctors about the firm. They don't think the stress is good for you.'

She was trying to judge my reactions, but I really had none.

'They've advised me to run the business down. I thought we might have a look at the books together.'

She gave me one. I tried to hold it, but my hands were shaking too badly and I had to lay it out on my lap. I looked it over.

'Bit of a mess,' I said, with a hint of a shrug.

'Yes, but we can sort it out.'

'I don't know when I last collected from these people.'

'I've done a lot of them.'

I looked at her in genuine surprise. 'You have?'

'But I've no idea what else is due in.'

'How much do we owe?'

'About seven thousand,' she replied flatly. 'No, Eric. Now don't worry. There'll be a solution . . .'

But I'd pushed the book away, and refused to look at it again that afternoon.

Knowing we were in debt to the tune of £7000 – twice as much as I'd embezzled – had fired my old fear with a new intensity. At least in Crumlin Road I'd had a future, some prospect of building a new life when I was let out; but here my imprisonment was twofold, for not only was I kept here by others – all I had to look forward to was bankruptcy. Night after night I would pace the dimly lit corridors of the hospital making futile calculations on the income required to retrieve my lost status. They all worked out more or less the same – £120 a week before I could afford even a single drink, let alone the rest. I might as well face it. My days of high living were over and I'd never see them again.

The thought followed me back to my room at dawn, where I'd sit in the easy chair for a moment or two, restlessly folding and unfolding my arms before getting to my feet again and pacing round the room. Every so often I'd pause in front of the iron frame of the window and gaze at the featureless grey squares of sky. Really all I wanted to do was drink – it was my only consolation. And if it got the better of me again, as it almost certainly would, well, there would always be another chance at the river. It still seemed the best way out.

Only one other person visited me. The first time he came he looked in at the door and said in a gentle, melodious voice, 'Hello. Remember me?'

'George Averly.'

We shook hands.

'I hope I'm not intruding . . .'

'Of course not. I don't get a lot of visitors.'

'Last time I saw you I got chased out of the house, as I recall,' he said, brushing off his hat as he sat down on the chair.

'Did you?' I couldn't remember it.

'Never mind. It's been a long time. You remember when you used to call at my house to collect insurance when your dad was ill?'

'That's going back.'

'My boy still talks about the time you played together at Lurgan. Glad he was in my team and not the other one, he says. You were quite a hooker.'

'They were good days.'

He smiled. 'They seem good, looking back. Maybe we wouldn't want to live them again.'

'Or maybe we would . . .'

'Ay. But what is it they say? Time waits for no man?'

I drew my eyebrows together in a faint gesture of assent, and gazed at the polished tiled floor and the reflection of the window. The man's quietness seemed to have filled the room; the only thing that moved in this gentle still life were my fingers, twitching and rattling like a pennant at the top of a mast.

George stayed for half an hour, then leaned forward and put his hat back on.

'Well, I must be going. Do you mind if I pop back in to see you, say, the day after tomorrow?'

I didn't mind at all.

'Oh, I just want to leave a wee verse with you, Eric,' he said, opening his pocket Bible to read what he clearly knew by heart. 'That's in Colossians three, seventeen.'

I got to like George's visits. He was very different from the proper, slightly curt man I'd collected insurance from in my teens; age had mellowed him, taken the flame from his eyes and left them warm and soft. Why he gave up so much of his time to visit me I couldn't have said – and often joked with him that he was making an excuse out of our rather distant family connection to do his work as a church elder. But he was never overbearing or preachy, and seemed to take it in good humour that the price of his reading verses to me was that I would ignore them. We always parted on good terms.

It was when he left on October 13th, 1976, that he pressed a small booklet into my hand. 'You might find it interesting,' he said.

I glanced at the cover, saw the word 'Bible' and laid it on the bedside cabinet.

'Now, just a wee verse, Eric. "The eternal God is thy refuge, and underneath are the everlasting arms." That's from Deuteronomy thirty-three, twenty-seven.' He put his hat on.

'Will Olive be coming up tonight?'

'Not till tomorrow. She's decorating.'

'Well, perhaps I'll pop back and see you tomorrow afternoon.'

Before that he'd come every other day, but I didn't mind; it just seemed peculiar – as if I were terminally ill and if he left it too long I might slip away. As soon as he left I got up off the bed and began my nightly round of pacing, first in my room, then in the corridor, stopping only to make myself yet another cup of coffee. I was making the same calculations I'd made the night before and the night before that, exploring all the nooks and crannies of my situation like a caged animal looking for a gap in the bars. There was none. At five in the morning I returned to my room and sat down. But I couldn't sit still. All I could hear in my head was George gabbling his latest verse: the eternal God is thy refuge, and underneath are the everlasting arms, the eternal God is thy refuge, and . . .

Finally out of sheer boredom I picked up the booklet and studied the cover.

# Science and the Bible

an
address
by

## Mr Ulric Jelinek

of the

## Severna Manufacturing Company of East Orange, N.J.

An address on anything by someone called Ulric Jelinek didn't hold out much promise. As for science and the Bible, that bout had been stopped in the first round. Mr Brien had known thirty years ago that scientific theories like evolution had made a nonsense of the Bible. Had Neil Armstrong seen God when Apollo 11 went to the moon? No. And if God wasn't to be seen in space, where was he? The answer seemed plain to everyone but the dimwitted people who still had the nerve to insist the Bible was 'true'. The same people who quarrelled like dogs over whether you should go to a football match or drink a pint of Guinness. The hypocrites.

At that point I almost put the booklet down again, but boredom made me turn the first page and almost immediately I came on something that surprised me:

'The Bible and science must interpret each other, you see, because God wrote them both. Since God wrote the Bible and the "book of science" there can be no disagreement between them. And if there is any disagreement in our minds between them you will find that is either because there is something wrong with the observation of the facts, or the interpretation of that observation.'

Whatever else he was, Ulric Jelinek seemed to be no fool. His argument, which was perfectly rational, was presented in the full confidence that he knew what he was talking about. I read on.

'In Jeremiah (33:22) there is a very simple statement: "The host of heaven cannot be numbered." Yet 450 years after Jeremiah made this statement, Hipparchus, the great scientist of his day, said there were exactly 1,026 stars in the universe. One hundred and fifty years later at the time of Christ, Ptolemy, the great Roman scientist, said there are not 1,026 stars in the universe, but 1,056. He may have looked up on a clearer night, I don't know. But 1,610 years later a fellow by the name of Galileo invented a little glass and looked up and said , there are more stars than this. As men have developed better instruments, they have discovered more stars; and as a matter of fact they now tell us that in our own galaxy there are 270 *billion* stars. A couple of years ago I spoke to a group of men at Grand Rapids and I said that we had about 2 million galaxies and I was right up to date. Two months later in the National Geographic a report on a new two hundred inch telescope said there are not 2 million galaxies, but *trillions* of them. And now we officially say that "The host of heaven cannot be numbered." We have just caught up with Jeremiah.'

I suddenly realised that my pulse was racing.

'Now if you got into a rocket ship and travelled at 186,000 miles a second, the speed of light, how far would you be in five minutes? As you travel from the centre of our galaxy at that speed it would take you 35,000 years to reach were the sun is, and that's only one third of the distance. If you wanted to continue on to the outside of the wheel to our nearest neighbouring galaxy, you would have to travel for 900,000 years. Someone said, "Do you think God is going to let man conquer space?" I said, Of course, he can go as far as he wants to. But how far can you go? Who wants to travel at 186,000 miles a second for 900,000 years? Where would you be? You would only be in the next galaxy, and you would be pretty old by the time you got back. And there are trillions of such galaxies . . .'

The sheer immensity of the universe was incomprehensible to me. I'd never dreamed of it before. No wonder Armstrong hadn't seen God when he landed on the moon: he hadn't seen any more of the universe than a flea sees of the world nestling in a dog's ear. And if the universe was as big as that, what could lie beyond it? I felt the hairs prickling on the back of my neck. The whole thing was staggering; and it wasn't just large – it was organized.

'. . . Another interesting statement, in Genesis (8:22) is, "While the earth remaineth, seedtime and harvest, and cold and heat, summer and winter and day and night shall not cease." The seasons must come in their time, God says. The sun and the moon and the stars function according to the ordinances God has put there. And what makes the seasons? The revolution of the earth around the sun. It is spinning on its axis at a rate of 1,000 miles an hour, and it is travelling with the sun at the rate of 780 miles an hour. Three directions at the same time, and in one direction alone it covers between five and six hundred million miles in one year. And if it lost only five seconds every million miles the seasons would be six months out of kilter from Adam's time until now. But God said, No, the seasons must come in their time. In all its travels the earth doesn't lose more than a thousandth of a second in a hundred years. And we think we know something about precision . . .'

So what did all this mean?

'God is no less exacting in the spiritual than he is in the scientific. Jesus Christ did not say "I am *a* way." He said "I am *the* way." You come to God on his terms. New let me press this home to you; it is not the church or the denomination you belong to, the job you have, the money you give to philanthropic organisations, the time you spend in Christian activities, that will get you anywhere. You cannot develop by this principle. There is nothing the natural man can do to become spiritual. God said you have got to come on his terms. And when I came on his terms and I recognised myself as a sinner before God, I received the Lord Jesus Christ as my saviour. And this has changed the entire course of my life . . .'

I put the booklet down. The first thing I felt was the sort of dizzy sensation you get riding a motorcycle over rough ground. I was experiencing what I'd never experienced before – the universe in its full and incredible splendour; yet not just the universe, but something even more resplendent, something so bottomless and powerful that the universe itself faded into nothingness before it. Suddenly there were no wayside bushes, no excuses, no jokes, no successes or failures to hide behind. Even the years separating me from my childhood turned transparent; only two things remained – I myself, and the terrible majesty of God. These two alone really existed. The rest – all I had taken until now to be the real world – was sheer illusion. Whatever meaning my life possessed consisted only and entirely in what had taken place between me and this awful, unimaginable Other. I could only bow my head beneath the judgement of God and know that I had blasphemed.

At that moment everything became very clear. The drink problem was nowhere in my mind. I saw myself standing before God as I knew one day I would have to stand, giving an account of my earthly life. It was a sorry tale. I had hated God; I had indulged my own appetites at the expense of my wife and family; I had lied; I had hurt others. Not all of it was visible to the outsider. Often enough I had passed off my failings as strengths and let other people admire them. My ego depended on that. But looked at now, looked at objectively, they seemed pathetic, absurd and miserably selfish. I wished I could dissociate myself from them, yet knew I could not. They clung. Instead, I fell on my knees and wept tears of repentance. 'God,' I said, 'I've made a mess out of this life. Please come into it and do whatever you want . . .'

The searchlight passed. But instead of the cold panic I had expected to feel I was left with reassurance and peace. *The eternal God is thy refuge, and underneath are the everlasting arms.* I could scarcely believe that to me, of all people, Almighty God should say such a thing. That he should be a refuge to a man who for two decades had sought refuge only in alcohol, and hold out his everlasting arms to catch one who had repeatedly and deliberately fallen from grace. And yet the peace was there within me as strong as a wall, more real than the chair I was sitting in. And that was only the beginning.

# 10:  A drinker reassembled

It was like coming out of a fever. By ten o'clock I'd had a good breakfast and felt completely calm. I was tired, but the inner peace was as powerful and pervasive as the fear it had replaced.

I soon realised something else had changed, too: for the first time in, I didn't know how long, I had no desire to drink. It wasn't the physiological addiction that went – I'd been free of that since they dried me out at the start of the treatment. It was the mental addiction, the overwhelming urge to take the easy way out of my problems. This amazed me, because my circumstances hadn't changed one iota. I still owed seven thousand pounds, and I was still in a psychiatric hospital with no prospect of a job and every chance of being declared bankrupt. So extraordinary was it that besides feeling immensely thankful I could hardly believe the experience was real. Like the old soldier, silence in the enemy trenches made me suspicious.

Olive must have felt the same way, because when I announced to her that I'd been 'saved' the night before she looked as if I'd sprouted an extra head.

'I don't believe it.'

'Well, nor do I, but it's happened. George was in last night and he left me this booklet. When I read it, well, everything seemed to click into place.' I gave a little laugh. 'It's just like the old Brethren preachers used to say. I gave my heart to the Lord. And now I feel different, a different person. There's no more urge to drink. Only this peace . . .'

Suddenly I didn't know whether I wanted to laugh or cry. Olive hesitated, then came forward and put her arms around me. We embraced in silence. Then she drew back, pulling a handkerchief from her purse.

'I'd been praying for this. We've all been praying for it.'

'It's taken me too long . . .'

'Eric, you do mean it, don't you? I pray that you mean it.'

I took her in my arms again. 'Of course I mean it. We're going to have a new start. A *real* new start.'

'You remember when I came out to get you at the river?'

'Yes.'

'When I was driving out and I didn't know what had happened to you? I knew the Lord was in the car with me. It was like he was really sitting in the seat next to me. He helped me get to you. I'd never told you that.'

'I wouldn't have listened.'

'No, you wouldn't.'

Some things words cannot express. I clasped her to me. I think I said, 'I'm so sorry for all I've done . . .'

'It doesn't matter. Not if it's going to change. You really don't want to drink?'

'Really.'

She dabbed her eyes with her handkerchief.

'The children will be thrilled.'

'I don't feel I know them.'

'You've got four,' she laughed. 'And they're all Christians.'

'So I'm last in the gate.'

But at the thought of my family I felt a faint tinge of anxiety.

'Do you think things are going to work out—with money?'

'We'll just have to pray,' said Olive.

She told the children that night. They were all delighted; Heather burst into tears. Finally convinced after a second visit that I meant what I'd said, Olive renewed her own commitment to the Lord, and we became, for the first time ever, a Christian family.

After my conversion I made rapid progress at the hospital and was discharged on November 11th with my sense of peace undiminished, but feeling emotionally fragile and, against all my expectations, terribly self-conscious. Like Crumlin Road, the psychiatric hospital had been a safe retreat from prying eyes and mischievous tongues, and I was loath to leave it. Back home in Lurgan I was the dreadful alcoholic who'd been taken into care. People looked at me and talked about me. But if I wanted to stay out of sight the only way to do it was to stay in the house.

By the first Saturday at home I was so fed up with being cooped up inside that I decided to brave the crowd and watch Lurgan—my old rugby team—playing at the Lane. Though the ground was a mere three hundred yards from the house it could only be reached down an alley, and one so narrow that I'd have been immediately recognisable to a passer-by. After wrestling with my conscience I decided to risk taking the car. I was half way through the first half when I saw in the driving mirror a police car drawing up behind. There was a tap on the window.

'This your car, sir?'

I nodded, my limbs rigid.

'Can I see your licence.'

'I don't have one. My daughter drove me here.'

112

'I see. Would you mind telling me where you live, sir?'

I complied abjectly. It had been a pointless lie. I watched the police car swing off into the alley, tried unsuccessfully to enjoy the rest of the first half, and when I couldn't, got out of the car and hurried home.

'It's okay,' said Olive as I came in the door.

'No it's not. I feel like it's all starting again.'

'We can sort it out.'

'How?'

'I'm going down to the police station.'

'It won't work.' I ran my fingers nervously through my hair.

'Now don't start pitying yourself.'

'Who told them?'

'We do have a reserve policeman living next door. You might have remembered that.'

'I don't want to go back to court. I couldn't face it . . .'

'And I don't want you wallowing in self-pity and going down to the club. Understand?'

I looked her in the face. She was anxious, but determined. I shook my head. 'It's all right. I don't want to drink, anyway.'

'Take an aspirin and lie down on the settee until I get back. I'll ask the kids to stay around.'

Clifford turned on the television and sat down with me to watch the horse racing. But if my eyes were at Newmarket my mind was sitting nervously in Lurgan police station while Olive argued uselessly with the Inspector. My instincts had been right – nothing good lasted long. I'd reached the first fence and fallen at it. I might be able to survive cocooned in the safe routines of a psychiatric hospital, but put me back in the real world and things would go wrong just as they had before, and probably with the same results. Once you were on the

113

circuit of alcoholism you kept going round and round till you dropped.

The racing gave way to athletics and athletics to soccer results. Just before the news Olive arrived home.

'You're off the hook.'

'No!'

'The Inspector's a Christian. When I told him you'd just been converted, and that you lied automatically, he said he'd let it pass.'

'He might *say* that.'

'He meant it. He wants to help you.'

'We'll see about that when we get the summons.'

She took my hand. 'Eric, there will be no summons. This is the Lord answering our prayers. Like George said: thy refuge, and underneath are the everlasting arms.'

Two weeks later I knew she was right. Inspector Cobb had a compassion I'd never before associated with the police. A short time later he was murdered by the IRA.


We went back to the account books, but only for short periods because I still had the shakes and my concentration was very poor. One night the telephone rang.

'You get it,' I said quickly.

Olive glanced at me and left the room. Two minutes later she returned.

'Maurice Peters. Apparently we bought some welding accessories off him.'

'How much?'

'Ten pounds.'

I laid my pen down. 'It's no good.'

'Don't worry, Eric.'

'Well look at all these,' I said, picking up a sheaf of unpaid bills. 'And goodness only knows how many more there are coming. How on earth are we going to pay them all?'

'We've just got to take one day at a time.'

'We're going to go bankrupt. We owe £7000 .'

'No we're not. I squared up the sales accounts yesterday.' Olive pushed the sales book over the table and ran a finger down the column of figures. 'According to this we have nine thousand due to come in.'

'And who's going to collect it?'

'I will.'

I sighed. 'Well that's good. That's very good.'

'So what's bothering you?'

'I suppose it all seems a bit hopeless.'

'Avoiding bankruptcy is *hopeless?*'

'No, no. I'm very thankful for that. And I'm thankful I haven't been as terrified of it since I was saved.'

'So?'

'It's just that we've still got to live after the firm's wound up.'

'We will.'

'Olive, I've done my calculations over and over again. We need a hundred and twenty pounds a week just to get by. And how much do we get from social security?'

'Forty-four.'

'Right.'

'We'll have to make savings, that's all.'

'But we shouldn't have to do that. We're a decent family, and we deserve a decent family income.'

'And you can't get a job, is that it?'

'Not the sort I should have to support you.'

Olive picked up the bills. 'Well, there's no use talking about that now. We'll take one day at a time, okay?'

I shrugged. 'All right. And what happens when the next creditor phones up?'

'He won't.'

'Olive, be practical . . .'

'Because we'll phone him first of all. We know we've got enough money coming in to cover the payments. All we have to do is call our creditors, explain what's happened, and ask for time to service our debts.'

'You're going to *tell* people we're in debt?'

'Why not?'

'Not even the family knows . . .'

'So what's the big secret?'

I'd never done business that way before. But I swallowed my pride. 'You think it'll work?'

'It will if we ask the Lord to help us.'

She sorted out the most urgent bills for immediate payment and deferred the rest. It all seemed to work out. But next morning a letter arrived from Maurice Peters Ltd demanding immediate payment of ten pounds with a threat of court action in the case of default.

'Now what?' I said, shoving the red notice into Olive's hand.

'Now we pay this from money earmarked for other bills, and pray we get the cash in time to pay them.'

'It could take months to squeeze money out of people. After the oil crisis they'll all have battened down the hatches.'

'We've just got to trust the Lord, Eric. Now come on, we'll go out and do the shopping.'

We came back to find a blank envelope pushed through the letter box. There was no note or signature inside – only two five pound notes. Olive allowed herself a little smile as she put them into her purse. It was George's verse proved right again, and a reminder that we were on the right lines.

I'd known from the moment the delegation visited me in hospital that I wouldn't be welcome back at the club. Renewing old friendships that way would hardly have been good for me, anyway, and since I no longer had any interest in drinking, socially or otherwise, there was little reason to return. For better or worse, though, my friends at the club were the only friends I'd had, and leaving them made me glad of Olive and the children because without a family the loneliness would have been all but unbearable. The fact was that coming out of alcoholism made me very dependent on other people's support. Ironically it also had the effect of driving other people away, for as I quickly realised the alcoholic remains *persona non grata* long after he has reformed. Even at the church, George Averly and the minister were the only ones to receive me with more than a cool handshake. Attending the morning service I felt as out of place as a leper at the Queen's garden party.

It was at church one day that the Boys' Brigade captain took me aside.

'I wanted a word with you about Clifford.'

'Is something wrong?'

'Not at all. He's been in the Boys' Brigade here for years now, and he's been a real asset. You know he's got together a silver band?'

'That was 1974.'

'It's going well. But he has a bit of trouble keeping order. Did I hear from Olive that you play the trombone?'

'You want *me* in the band?'

He patted my shoulder. 'Not exactly. I wondered if you'd like to get involved with the BB, and look after the music from the business end. Uniforms, instruments, trips, that sort of thing.'

He knew before he'd finished asking me that he'd hit

the mark. He introduced me to the battalion president, David Johnson, and I started at the BB the following week. In the circumstances nothing could have been better to restore my shattered confidence and fulfil my need of companionship. At last I had a niche in the church where I felt at ease; and if the challenges of the work – like cooking for the BB camp – would have been a joke to me ten years before, at that time they were just what I needed to give me a fresh sense of accomplishment. For twelve months I divided my time between the BB, reading, and the family. We had so little money I had to sell the car, but I didn't mind. I was happier than I'd ever been before.

By 1978 I felt I'd recovered sufficiently to start looking for a job. But after thirty-four applications I wasn't asked for a single interview. This galled me because I knew for a fact that for some of the posts I was the best qualified applicant, and I decided to phone up the DHSS to find out what was going on. The official was at a loss until I told her I'd spent time in a psychiatric hospital. When I asked her if that made me unemployable she admitted cautiously that it was a 'factor'. She promised to get back to me but never did. The psychiatrist I consulted was more candid: have a record of psychiatric treatment, he said, and a lot of potential employers will strike you off the list.

I was furious, then frustrated, then sorry for myself.

'But we're getting along okay,' said Olive.

'We can't live on social security for ever.'

'But there's no hurry.'

'It's not right, is it? I have a wife and a family. I ought to be earning a good wage, not relying on the state. How is it that a next door neighbour of ours has a good job and he's not even a Christian?'

'I don't see why you're so upset about it.'

'Well look at the house. It needs repainting. How are we going to afford that?'

'Jesus didn't have a house.'

'What does that have to do with it?'

'I'm saying being a Christian doesn't entitle you to a big wage. Not as I see it, anyway. Isn't that what the minister said last Sunday, that we should be like Jesus?'

I frowned. 'Yes. He did.'

Since I had a lot of free time on my hands I decided I'd try and find out what sort of life Jesus led. A read through the Gospels surprised me. Jesus hadn't made compromises: he'd been more critical of the religious leaders of his day than I'd been of the men and women at my father's assembly. He had no compunction about calling the Pharisees hypocrites, and he drove the money changers out of the temple with a whip. The demands he made on his followers were so absolute they were virtually impossible to obey. Who after all had ever loved God with his entire heart, soul, body and mind, or loved other people as much as he loved himself? Yet Jesus actually led by example. He lived with the poor and washed the feet of his disciples; and – Olive was quite right – he did not own a house. He didn't seem to have had anything at all except the clothes he stood up in.

I remembered the man I'd heard a long time ago preaching on the virtues of poverty, and leaving the little church in Donacloney in a Jaguar. There were a lot of men like that in the church. Probably there always had been. Consequently the world was as unjust and divided as it had been when Jesus went to the cross. What sort of place would it be if Christians really practised the sort of faith Jesus preached? What sort of place would Northern Ireland be? It was just as I was asking myself these kind of questions that I happened to read Ronald Sider's *Rich Christians in an Age of Hunger*. It shook my values down to the foundation. For the first time I was seeing my own problems in perspective. How on earth could I justify seeking a big salary to pay for things that in terms of the world's needs were a useless extravagance? I couldn't. But of course it was all very well to *say* it . . .

'We want that job,' said Olive firmly.

I looked at the small print under her finger. The presbyterian church in Donacloney was offering £7.50 a week for a sexton.

'Are you crazy?'

'I think we should go for it.'

'You know what a sexton does? He digs graves. You want me to take seven and a half pounds home at the end of the week for doing that?'

'We've got to start somewhere, Eric. You didn't get a big appointment, so we'll apply for a small one.'

She was resolute, and in the end I agreed to enquire, consoling myself that with thirty-four failed applications behind me a thirty-fifth was inevitable. It turned out I was the only one interested.

So it was that in 1979 after twenty-three years away, the high-flier who'd landed that job in Omagh came back to earth with a bump. Things could have been worse. The sexton's post had a pretty little tied cottage and given a reasonable turnover of funerals you could earn quite a bit in bonuses. But for me far outweighing any of these benefits was the odium of returning to Donacloney's tight knit social circle and having to endure the slow assassination of gossip. I'd rather have walked on hot coals than suffer this mockery of a prodigal's return, the covert glances, the mute shaking of heads. It brought back too many painful memories of childhood; in fact it was like being subjected to the frustrations of childhood all over again, for on top of everything else, when I'd sworn to leave the village and its strictures behind me for ever, there was the ultimate humiliation of being proved wrong.

# 11: Home from home

Gravedigging's an unenviable occupation. Sometimes on a wet day when the walls of the trench cave in and you're standing deep in muddy water you wonder why you're doing it. But there are pleasant interludes – lawns to be cut and flowerbeds to be tended. And outside you occasionally see those sunsets in which for a fleeting moment past and present seem reconciled and the world at peace, though a peace defined by the orderly arrangement of tombs may seem to you rather grim.

My father's grave lay thirty yards or so from the stone hut where I kept my tools. I had trimmed the grass around it countless times before one evening, I went back and sat quietly on the railings of the next tomb, and looked at it.

'Hello, Father.'

I glanced over my shoulder, and fell silent again, staring at the ground between my boots. Eventually I took a deep breath and went on, carefully, like a sick man dictating a letter.

'I don't think I understood, when I was a boy, what it was you went through here. Mother told me, after you died, what happened when you lost your job at the mill. Why you took work selling insurance. How you were forced to move. Those must have been terrible days. I've never seen days like that. To me this was just – home. Where we lived. I'd heard about the Linen Lords, but I'd never worked for them. Never had to load all I owned on to a pony and van and move because of them . . .

'I know now you wanted to save us from all that. That's why you sent us to school and drove us so hard. So we wouldn't have to work for the Linen Lords, the way you had to. Nothing mattered more to you than lifting us out of the hole they'd put you in. You worked hard for that . . . and you expected us to work hard too. You believed we would see things the way you did . . . Did you ever find out all of my secrets? All the football matches I went to, the cigarettes I smoked, the drinks? You probably did, finally, when I went to prison. What that must have done to you . . . And you know something? I blamed it all on you. Blamed it all on my father.'

I sighed, and felt my throat tightening. 'Well, I think I've finally grown up. I went straight, in the end. I went back to Olive like you wanted me to. I just wanted to tell you that—I'm sorry. I only wish I'd said it before.'

I got to my feet, drew a forearm across my eyes and picked up the trimmers.

To sit and talk to my father made me realise I'd carried a profound sense of guilt since his death. Finally apologising went some way to dispelling it, but I was left with a dissatisfaction, and a desire to prove myself that was at one and the same time a restitution for my past life and a continuation of it. I wanted nothing better than to escape from Donacloney and perform some great work. Perhaps not the founding of another business—after my meditations on the life of Christ that seemed shallow and egocentric—but a great moral work, something that would help the disadvantaged, people lost in alcoholism as I had been. The force of this desire was undeniable, but I didn't recognise its source until on one grey afternoon in December something happened that showed it up as clear as day.

One of my duties as sexton was to attend funerals, which meant looking sombre and official and scattering a spadeful of dirt into the grave I'd dug a couple of days before, while the minister read the 'Dust to dust and ashes to ashes.' I always felt a bit self-conscious, and on this particular occasion I decided to get my own back by looking up during the prayers to see how many of these locals were really praying. I let my eyes wander insolently along the line of mourners. Then I went rigid – she was looking straight at me, and giving me a crooked, slightly sneering smile.

I looked down abruptly; I didn't know who this woman was, but I was embarrassed at her blatant exhibition of scorn. More than that, I was angry. That smile said everything Donacloney thought about Eric Lennon; it could hardly have been any clearer if she'd stepped over the grave and slapped me in the face. But while I stood smarting from the insult I heard someone speaking to me. It wasn't the minister. It wasn't anybody in the graveyard.

'What are you worried about?' the voice said.

I would have opened my eyes a second time if I hadn't known instinctively who said it. There was, I suddenly realised, no doubt at all what I was worried about – I'd been worried about it for most of my life and hadn't stopped worrying when I became a Christian. It was my reputation. I felt so angry with that woman because she'd wounded my pride. I really did feel a cut above the average resident of Donacloney, and resented having to work as their sexton, as though I were a king being made to dress in rags. At that moment it became acutely obvious why God had brought me here. This pride was so deeply rooted that Donacloney was the only surgery capable of removing it. This funeral was my consultation with the surgeon. I could almost hear the rustle of paper as a form of consent was pushed over the desk for me to sign.

'Well?' said the voice.

I gave in. There would be no more hunting for the most prestigious position. I wasn't to give myself airs. When I applied this time it was for a job I wouldn't have looked twice at before. In fact the first to come up was a night-shift in a bakery, and as though the point needed emphasis I didn't even get this – the sort of job most employers would struggle to fill – without supplying a reference. This put me on the spot because although I was reluctant to ask the minister I couldn't think of anyone else who could honestly say I was a straight, hard-working and trustworthy person. That I finally decided on the battalion president was fortunate because he immediately offered me a slightly better-paid position in his own firm, as night watchman. I accepted with relief and gratitude.

It seemed strange that after months and years of failure trying to set myself up with the wage I thought I needed, security came only when I gave up working things out for myself and left them in the hands of God. And to be honest I didn't do badly, either. One night at the warehouse I calculated our total weekly earnings, and found that by saving £20 on a residential post as sexton and receiving £16 disability allowance from the DHSS for Isobel, Olive's and my wages together brought in £118.50 – almost exactly the sum I'd despaired of earning as I paced the corridors in the psychiatric hospital.

Three months later the firm was wound down and I was made redundant, but there was no problem getting work this time. In fact I had two offers made directly to me – a two year Youth and Community Diploma course at the Belfast Polytechnic, and a post as Organising Secretary at the Belfast Simon Community. I would dearly have loved to take the course at the Poly, but I knew it would involve a three month placement in Germany, and would only have started me on the ladder of social success I'd vowed to leave behind. I did what I knew was the right thing, and accpeted the job at the Simon Community caring for the down-and-outs. I often say it was a job for which I served a twenty-five year apprenticeship.

I hadn't been at the Simon Community long when on the way out of church one Sunday morning Clifford came dashing up and grabbed me by the arm.

'Dad, you're wanted on the phone. It's urgent.'

We began to jog back together.

'Who is it?'

'I think it's the police.'

'Has something happened?'

'It's Uncle Wallace – he's been abducted by the IRA.'

'He's *what?*'

I paused to stare at Clifford for a second, then strode into the house to pick up the phone. It was true – a statement from the IRA said he was being 'held for questioning'. There could be little doubt what it really meant. As a reserve policeman Wallace was unlikely to be privy to any information useful to the provisionals; almost certainly he'd already been shot, and the body was being held in the hope of luring the security forces into a trap. For ten long days a thin thread of hope was spun out by the media. We sat by the phone, listening to every news broadcast, almost wishing that Wallace had been gunned down like John so we'd know he was dead instead of having to endure the awful waiting. When the phone finally rang it was what we'd expected to hear: a body discovered in the woods.

For the first time since my conversion my faith was

really shaken. Why had God let this happen to a man like Wallace? Why had two people from the same family been so senselessly destroyed? It made me angry and bitter. I had no urge to drown my sorrows in drink – with God's strength I could control that now – but I wanted to be alone with my grief, and during the next few days I went around sulking and refusing to pray. Then, on a warm summer night, I had a dream.

The heat of the silent explosion was so intense I thought it must have been a nuclear bomb. In a Belfast street the crowd flashed white and tumbled forward in confusion, trapping me in a mass of struggling bodies. *It's the IRA,* someone was yelling at me. I felt him thrust me down as he clambered away to make his escape. *Where are you going?* But he'd vanished, and the crowd was on its feet again and streaming away from the blast. I reached out for Olive and the children. They were all there. *It's a trap,* I said. *That last bomb was planted to drive us on to a bigger one.* But it was impossible to make headway against the tide of people running down the street; when you tried to push them out of the way your muscles seemed to freeze and you were carried further into danger. Suddenly there was another flash and a blast of heat. I smothered Olive with my own body and flung us down to the ground. When we rose – was it seconds or hours later? – we were in a city of ruins. Where the crowd had been running there now lay only a mass of charred embers, shapes vaguely recognisable as human, glowing red hot, and giving off profuse steam. We began to hurry this way and that looking for the children. Frantically I kicked the embers about, my clothes soaked through with sweat and vapour. Finally we found them – or what was left of them – and just stood, holding one another amid the ruins. I wondered if there was going to be a third blast. It didn't matter much now. I felt my breath heaving in and out, in and out. The steam was everywhere, and seemed to be closing up around us . . .

I jerked upright, lathered in sweat. Nothing glowed on the dark floor of the bedroom. The steam had gone, and outside the window under a quarter moon I could hear a cricket singing. I undid my pyjama jacket to lay a hand on my heart, then eased myself out of bed carefully, for fear of waking Olive, and stood at the window. The dream was still very near, though I couldn't see it; if I went back to sleep it would certainly return. I didn't want to sink back into it, so I stayed gazing out into the night, letting the breeze bring me to. I wasn't prone to nightmares. Why had it been so vivid? I mulled over the dream, and then I heard a voice, like the voice in the graveyard, say to me, 'Read Job.'

Before then I had rarely dipped into the Old Testament, but I went downstairs, found the Book of Job, and read all forty-two chapters in a single sitting. What had happened to Job, I concluded, was much like what had happened to me in the dream. He hadn't known about bombs but the worst disasters imaginable at the time had fallen on him. He too had lost everyone but his wife. But when he demanded to know why it had happened God more or less told him to mind his own business. Wasn't that a bit hard? It seemed that way; and yet there wasn't really anything God could have said to Job that would have satisfied him. The disasters that happen are the natural corollary of human freedom, God's greatest gift to men. Bad things happen not because God makes them happen but because men and women are free to act as they want to and sometimes, quite often in fact, that brings misery and destruction. I should have known that well enough from my own life. That accepted, the best thing you could do when evil befell you was to keep faith with God. To pray and not to sulk.

It was a lesson I could have done with learning a long time before; this time I took it to heart.

The Simon Community affected me profoundly in two ways. Among my first and strongest impressions of the community's residents was that they were poor; they were lost and lonely people who had often reached life's scrap-heap before they turned twenty, and had stayed there, disregarded and unemployable. But at the same time I knew this was a relative poverty. Deserving as they were of care and support, their poverty didn't deprive them of shelter, clothing and three square meals a day. Poor they might be by the affluent standards of Britain, but in global terms these derelicts who propped up the country's socio-economic scale were among the comparatively well-off. How many thousands of people overseas died every day for lack of food, shelter and adequate sanitation and medicine? Almost certainly more than Simon Communities provided for in the whole of the UK.

This reinforced the point made by Ronald Sider. Even when I'd made all the allowances for family responsibility and having to live in a place where costs as well as salaries were high, I still turned out to be embarrassingly rich. And in what sense could I claim the money I earned as my own, when the Bible taught very clearly that anything we have is kept in trust for our Creator? Shouldn't I be selling anything that wasn't absolutely essential for my family's welfare, to better the lot of the world's real poor? I concluded pretty fast that my values still needed some radical alteration if I was to follow Jesus Christ with any sort of integrity, and accordingly I resolved that in future I would be less concerned about my childrens' education, my holidays, security, possessions and home, and apply myself instead to the spiritual and material welfare of others, and to speaking out about the injustices in our society.

The second thing I learned at the Simon Community was that I didn't want to stay there. This wasn't because I got bored listening to the remorseful or bitter tales of old alcoholics – I just couldn't do anything for them. Urging reform on hardened addicts was a thankless task, and anyway the Simon policy was only one of containment. What I wanted was to get to people before they'd sunk too far – to work with the young. Naturally when I was offered a post as senior house parent in a government hostel for boys I jumped at it. But I didn't stay. I was too appalled. Young boys were actually being introduced to alcohol on the premises; staff were coming to work drunk; and cases of sexual assault on youngsters were covered up instead of being investigated. I'd been warned for my own good to keep quiet about what my colleagues called 'goings on' until my contract came up for renewal, but I refused and told them exactly what I thought about it. My contract was never renewed, and the place was closed down a month after I left.

Where the once fast-living, hard-drinking Eric Lennon finally ended up was on the Shankill Road.

I'd been doing a bit of part-time voluntary youth work for the Local Education Library Authority when I was offered the job of youth worker at Shankill Road Mission. The Mission has been there for a hundred years. It has always served the social needs of the area, and once provided, among other things, food, clothing, holidays, seaside trips and dental treatment. During the relatively affluent years of the fifties and sixties these old needs gradually disappeared. But new ones have taken their place. Unemployment. Glue sniffing. Alcohol abuse. Paramilitary involvement. And the Mission has met the challenge. It provides twenty-seven jobs by running a day centre and a clothes shop, and sends a team of assistants out into the community.

I've been working with the young people. It's a tough, unpredictable assignment in a dangerous area – hardly what I as a young man or any of my drinking companions would have considered 'success'. There's no big wage. No expense account or company car. No luxurious home. We live in a little flat with windows so high you can't see much but the sky. And yet I can say with complete honesty that I have never been happier. That's real happiness, not the sort I used to fake when I had a drink in my hand. It goes all the way down and it's with me all the time. Over the years I've known well about thirty hard drinkers in the province, and I doubt if any of them could say that. I know for a fact that twelve of them are dead – one committed suicide not long before I wrote this book. If that's success I'm glad to be counted among the 'failures'. Alcohol destroys the quality of life and cuts it short. But, thank God, there is a way out of the prison for those who really want their lives to be changed. It's not an easy way. God won't give an instant, push-button solution to the broken life of the alcoholic. But it is a complete solution, and I am eternally grateful that I found it.

# 12: A few sobering facts

For the last two chapters of this book I want to turn from my own story to the important issues raised by alcohol consumption in modern Britain.

Only very recently has the scale of the problem achieved anything like public recognition. That is long overdue for reasons that will soon become clear, and its delay is probably owing to the peculiar way drinking is regarded by the British people. Plainly, as in my own case, the last person to admit that his drinking is a problem is the drinker. His wife will know it all right, and so will his children. So also will the government, when his name appears in the drink-driving statistics or he lands up in jail. Nonetheless the prevailing opinion is that drinking is 'okay'. Unlike drug abuse drunkenness enjoys a large measure of social acceptability. *Yet three quarters of a million people in Britain are registered alcoholics.*

## What you're getting for your pint

Whether or not you're registered, of course, is beside the point. Alcohol is usually causing damage to the body long before the drinker sees it as a problem.

A documentary on alcohol in the 1985 series *O'Donnell Investigates** included an interview with a consultant

*I am indebted to the producers of this programme for much of the material used in this chapter.

physician working in an intensive care unit. The patient he was treating had collapsed with acute pancreatitis – inflammation of the pancreas gland – and was not expected to survive. Yet this man exhibited none of the behaviour patterns usually associated with major illness. He wasn't a heavy smoker, he wasn't grossly overweight. In a technical sense he wasn't an alcoholic – at five or six large measures of spirits in the working day and twenty-four over the weekend he was what society classes as a 'social' drinker. Nonetheless, alcohol was going to kill him.

There is a startling list of illnesses linked as closely to alcohol consumption as lung cancer is to smoking. Most people know that heavy drinking can cause cirrhosis and hepatitis – disorders of the liver – but who would associate it with gastritis, ulcers, blood pressure, brain damage, muscle disease, nervous and psychiatric disorders and cancer of the mouth, throat and gullet? Who for that matter would know – or care to admit – that drinking impairs his sexual performance or causes memory loss and muscular twitching? Yet the connection is undeniable.

Of course most drinkers would deny that they are 'heavy' drinkers, or that they are going 'over the top'. But the trouble with terms like 'heavy drinker', 'social drinker' and 'alcoholic' is that they conjure up an image of a certain sort of person rather than giving any precise information about the amount of alcohol consumed. The man who tells you he's a social drinker is really saying that he drinks but he's still okay. Like me, he will probably go on saying it when his friends and family know for a fact that drinking is getting him into serious trouble. So how much can you take on a regular basis without running the risk of illness?

As with smoking the answer depends on a lot of factors,

like your size, sex, age and general health, but the limit even for the young and fit is thirty-six standard drinks per week for a man, and twenty-four for a woman. (The difference between the sexes has to do with how much of the body's weight is made up of water, diluting the alcohol.) By a standard drink we mean simply a drink that contains a single unit of alcohol. A half-pint of beer, a glass of table wine, a glass of sherry and a single whisky each contain one unit of alcohol, so each is a standard drink. Beer, people often say, isn't as strong as spirits, but if you drink a pint of it you're still having two standard drinks – in other words as much alcohol as you'll get in a double whisky. By this reckoning a man can have two and a half pints of beer every night, or a woman three glasses of sherry, and avoid any long-term risk to their health.* That doesn't mean they can't be alcoholics – physical or psychological dependence can develop on as little as one glass of sherry a day – it just means they're unlikely to wind up with throat cancer or cirrhosis as a direct consequence of their drinking.

But major illness isn't in the end the main way that alcohol kills people. The drinker who is 'heavy' in the sense that he often goes over the medically safe limit will probably die in a car accident long before his liver packs in. The reason for this is the double effect of alcohol. Technically alcohol is a depressant – in other words it suppresses certain functions of the brain with the inevitable result that the car driver has slower reactions and reduced physical coordination. At the same time he will almost certainly feel more confident and 'loosened

---

*Even this may be an over-estimate. The Royal College of Psychiatrists, who previously set the 'low risk' limit at eight standard drinks per day, issued a report in 1986 reducing this limit to three standard drinks (one and a half pints of beer) for a man, and two units for a woman.

up', and more willing to take risks. Hardly surprising then that in 1984 a thousand drink drivers were killed and a further 98,000 convicted for road traffic offences.

In a sense the very existence of a 'legal limit' is misleading, because it implies that what is legal is harmless, which may be true when we distinguish borrowing from theft, but is a nonsense in the measurement of blood alcohol levels. A single drink impairs the judgement sufficiently to make accidents more likely; what the law has done is decide an arbitrary level at which the risk of accident becomes unacceptable. Tests have proved that if a man has two and a half pints of beer in one hour – the intake required on average to put his blood level at the legal limit of 80mg – his chances of crashing his car will have increased by four. But one pint will make him a more dangerous driver, no matter how hard he tries. At twice the legal limit (five pints) he'll have twenty-five accidents for every one he might have when he's sober.

The driver pulled in for suspected drink-driving may well protest that how much he drinks is his own business – and he will be quite right. The law only steps in because it is also the business of the passengers he is carrying, the other drivers on the road, and of the small children playing ball on the pavement. (At a total annual cost of ninety million pounds to the taxpayer drink-related accidents are ultimately everyone's business.) From this point of view the behavioural effects of alcohol are more immediate and serious than the long-term medical ones, for the recklessness and belligerence often produced by alcohol can, and frequently do, cause injury to an innocent third party. Witness the publicity given to the problem of controlling violence at football matches. But the problem is wider than that. Vandalism, street fighting and domestic violence, for instance, are most common between the hours of 10.00 pm and 2.00 am at weekends; half the known cases of domestic violence are attributed to the husband's drinking, and a report made by the Parole Board in 1980 put the proportion of alcohol related murders (calculated from the cases released the previous year) at fifty per cent – a figure they estimate to be much the same for all unpremeditated acts of violence. Besides this, according to the Royal College of Psychiatrists, alcohol is implicated in nineteen per cent of deaths by drowning, thirty per cent of deaths by fire, and forty-three per cent of fatal falls.

And the problem is getting worse. A magistrate interviewed on O'Donnell's programme stated that alcohol-related offences had risen by approximately twenty-five per cent during the seventies while consumption had gone up by thirty per cent. Again this view is corroborated by the Royal College of Psychiatrists, whose report claims that alcohol consumption in the UK has risen by fifty per cent since 1960 with 'devastating consequences for the health and well-being of the nation.' It is, to say the least, a little curious that in a society so concerned about the abuse of hard drugs the much more widespread effects of alcohol abuse should pass relatively unnoticed. As Dr Marcus Grant of the Alcohol Research Unit in Edinburgh has pointed out, 'In any one year alcohol causes ten to twenty times more problems than all the illegal drugs put together.'

## Prohibition and all that

The difference comes down in the end to the way people look at things.

A person will be encouraged to drink if his personal

circumstances predispose him to it and if drink is easily available. In the early years of this century both of these conditions were fulfilled in Britain. Pubs were open seventeen hours a day, poverty was widespread, and drink was the easy consolation. But at the same time there was a strong feeling, grounded in the religious convictions of the nation, that drink was a social evil, and so the temperance movement – with the Band of Hope and the Salvation Army at the fore – arose to press for the restriction of licensing hours. Since the social consequences of alcohol abuse were costly to the nation, it got a swift response. By 1914 even the Shipbuilders Employers' Federation – not an organisation noted for its teetotalism – were urging the government to restrict the sale of alcohol because absenteeism resulting from drink was seriously affecting production. 'We are fighting Germany, Austria and the drink,' said Lloyd George in the Commons, 'and as far as I can see the greatest of these is the drink.' In spite of the objections voiced by the licensed trade legislation was passed in 1915 to reduce pub opening to five and a half hours. Consumption fell by fifty per cent, and drink offences plummeted to one sixth of their pre-war level.

The Americans went a step further in 1919 by introducing prohibition, a policy that lasted for fifteen years and is obscurely associated with bootlegging and Al Capone style gangsterism. It was the gangsters, in fact, who did most to end it, by bringing pressure to bear on the big industrialists and thus on the Federal Government. But a recent study by Robin Rube, a Californian researcher, argues that the prohibition era does not deserve the scorn the media and film industry have poured on it. Like the British temperance movement it began with widespread popular support; it cut alcohol consumption by an estimated sixty-six per cent and dramatically reduced the incidence of cirrhosis and alcoholic psychosis. Politically and culturally it may have been a failure, but medically it worked.

By 1935 Britain did not have an alcohol problem of the scale that had existed in the early post-Victorian era. But from that date consumption of alcohol began to rise steadily. Between the mid-fifties and the mid-seventies it doubled, with a corresponding increase in social conflict, cirrhosis deaths, and hospital admissions for alcohol-related cancer. In response to this the last Labour government under James Callaghan commissioned a report on alcohol abuse from the Think Tank, which correctly identified the cause of increasing comsumption as increasing availability. Availability, of course, means more than the number of pubs and restaurants you can go to for a drink – it means also how much of it you can afford to buy. In 1938 a labourer earning the average national wage would have had to work for eight and a half hours to pay for one bottle of whisky; by 1960 the equivalent figure was six hours, and by 1976 it had dropped to two and a half. Similarly the pint of beer that 'cost' twenty-four minutes' work in 1938 could in 1976 be earned in a mere eleven minutes. Alcohol consequently became a growth industry: falling prices increased demand, which in turn increased production with a further fall in prices. And what did the Think Tank recommend? In short, decisive government action to break the cycle of increasing consumption by legislating against price cuts and, therefore, restricting availability.

The report's recommendations were never put into practice. In fact, O'Donnell could not squeeze from either of the major parties an admission that it had ever existed. (He only obtained it in the end because a copy of the suppressed report was somehow leaked and published in Sweden!) What did eventually appear in 1981 was a document issued by the Health Department entitled *Drinking Sensibly*. This candidly admitted most of the worst trends in alcohol abuse: that drinking convictions and admission to psychiatric hospitals for alcohol treatment had doubled between 1968 and 1978, that there was a connection between the rise in alcohol abuse and the rise in overall consumption, and that the comparative price of drink was no greater at the beginning of the eighties than it had been two decades before – a trend that the 1986 budget did nothing to reverse. But unlike its predecessor this publication made no bold demands on the government. In fact it excused the Chancellor from using his most effective weapon – the Inland Revenue – on the grounds that the blunt instrument of taxation would penalise the innocent drinker along with the potential alcoholic (though quite how you distinguish the two is never made clear). It urged greater publicity on the dangers of alcohol abuse, and initiatives at places of work to encourage problem drinkers to seek help.

Plainly this is a very different approach from that taken to drug abuse. There is plenty of publicity to discourage the use of heroin but in the end if you're found with any on you you're liable to prosecution. So what is the difference between heroin and alcohol? Medically very little: both are narcotics, both are addictive. We might add that both are profitable for their producers and distributors, and that both can be abused – the major difference here being one of scale as alcohol is far more widely available, far cheaper, far more ubiquitous in its effect on law and order, productivity and social breakdown, and far higher in its cost to the nation. 750,000 registered alcoholics is a lot of dead weight economically, never mind the unregistered ones. Combine this with the cost to the NHS of treating alcohol-related illness, the cost of man-hours lost through absenteeism and inefficiency, and the long-term cost of secondary effects like family breakdown and disturbed children, and you've got yourself a king-size problem. Yet alcohol is still legal, and the government is content with a few gestures in the direction of education against abuse, on the utterly unfounded assumption that drinking will be basically harmless for all but a number of individuals who 'can't handle it'. What's going on?

## What you don't know could kill you

The most obvious reason for government inaction is that the sale of alcohol brings in billions of pounds a year in tax revenue. But the complexity of the relationship between government and industry means there is more to the issue than miserliness at the Exchequer. For one, many Members of Parliament have direct interests in the alcohol trade, or have influential constituents who do, with the inevitable result that there is inertia in the House whenever legislation is proposed to restrict sales. No one will admit to this; they will be far more likely to point out that legislation aiming at reducing overall consumption of alcohol – by restricting availability or increasing taxes and forcing producers to put up the price – will have the effect of needlessly crippling an otherwise healthy industry and putting another section of the population out of work. It will be mortgaging the present for the sake of the future – something democratic politics has never been good at because an electorate, understandably, wants jam today, not jam tomorrow.

Which brings us back to the point that the difference

between effective legislation and pious bumbling is the way people – the electorate – look at things. Sixty years ago enough of them looked on alcohol as being the clear cause of unhappiness and decline to galvanise the government into doing something about it. Where is that lobby today? It is a minority. You might almost say a despised minority, since to society at large terms like temperance and teetotal – once banners of a movement as popular in its day as the one now for racial equality – smack of stern moralism and Victorian prudery. In the progressive world of the 1980s the man who refuses a drink is apt to be regarded as a crank.

This shift from real issues to 'associations' or 'images' is characteristic of the advertising media. The drinker may chide his teetotal friend, but he himself is equally influenced by an image busily promoted by the drinks industry that links the act of consuming alcohol with good looks, youth, sporting activity, camaraderie and sex. That the average man at the bar is spotty, insecure and about as attractive to his girlfriend after a night's boozing as a beached walrus, hardly enters into it. The media have invested drinking with desirable associations that flatter the potential client in order to achieve the supplier's goal, which is to increase demand. In the glitzy atmosphere of the modern bar the nervous acned youth feels himself transformed from a social frog into a prince charming: he becomes, as long as the spell lasts, part of the cherished in-crowd. But this small delusion, shared by all regular drinkers, leads ultimately to the dangerous paradox of belligerent and facile behaviour. The brawls and drinking competitions the adverts discreetly leave out, are what the drinker is conditioned to see as the 'good life'. For a large number it will go all the way and finish with the pathetic scene of the man or woman who has graduated to *other* in-crowds (in jail, in debt, in hospital, in the morgue) still vigorously denying that he is alcoholic. Such is the power of the media to gild the pill.

Naturally those among the electorate who stand to gain by this arrangement cannot be expected to take the initiative in changing it. No off-licence owner will go out of his way to ask for proof of a young person's age, and no publican or club manager with a healthy business sense will press for shorter drinking hours. The trend has rather been for licensed establishments to encourage drinking by laying on games and giant TV screens, or in the case of some hotels, entertainment for the kids while mum and dad spend lunchtime at the bar. That is to be expected. But what is truly surprising is how far this permissive attitude to drinking has spread throughout society as a whole. The drinker who kills someone in a road accident will generally be viewed as a *social* drinker even if, like me, he was plainly an alcoholic – he'd just gone 'a bit over the top' on New Year's Eve and done something silly that in his right mind he'd never think of. And this indulgent attitude to heavy drinking isn't just a matter of public opinion: it goes all the way down to our legal system, for if a homicide can show that he committed the act under the influence of alcohol that is still in Britain accepted as a mitigating circumstance! The simple fact is that the British people would rather excuse alcohol abuse than stop it.

That we have reached this situation little more than half a century after the great temperance campaigns has a lot to do with a general slide into relative morals and an ill-defined belief that 'you should be able to do what you like provided it doesn't hurt anyone else.' Of course, which end of this statement has greater importance depends on who it's applied to. Anyone who lives near a nuclear reactor will probably dispute the government's right to 'do what it wants' even if the solid evidence of harm caused by radiation is relatively small. And yet to the drinker the fact that a thousand deaths every year result directly from the influence of alcohol will seem a poor reason for someone else to step in and control his drinking. He will probably regard it as an infringement of his rights if his driving licence is removed for an offence of which he is indisputably guilty. That is about all the 'provided it doesn't hurt anyone else' clause counts for when the chips are down.

This defensive mood inevitably leaves its mark on the younger generation. In fact in the course of his upbringing a young person's basic attitudes to the alcohol question will probably be formed – often without any explicit exchange of information – long before he gets any formal education on the subject. If he grows up in a drinking home he will adopt his parents' values from the start; if he grows up in a self-consciously non-drinking home he may well adopt them as a form of self-assertion during his teens. Either way he is very unlikely to be told the facts about alcohol – that it is a narcotic drug that kills people and causes crippling dependence – simply because his parents don't know the facts, or are incapable of discussing the issue on any other level than that of personal prejudice. (In my experience it is increasingly the case that the parents' unwillingness to admit their own failures to the growing child is a major cause of communication breakdown in the early teens, and of the child being forced out, without any sort of guidance, to investigate the world of alcohol and drugs for himself.) By the time a young person reaches secondary school and learns the facts it is frequently too late. And that is, anyway, assuming that the school even teaches them – an assumption by no means justified in a country where the total expenditure on education against abuse is a meagre one-and-a-half million pounds.

When the young person enters adult life the pressures are nearly all towards drinking. Universities, far from exercising restraint, often issue new students with free beer tickets, and this helps establish drinking as a social habit. (I've had students referred to me by magistrates in the hope that a tour of skid row will cure a developing drink problem.) Things don't improve at work. Unfortunately it's a fact that in many places you have to go to the pub just to meet people socially, and once you're there, peer pressure will almost certainly ensure that you drink. Drinking is after all what parents, media and friends all agree to be the essential ingredient of the 'good life'.

If the social habit passes through alcohol abuse to dependence the miseducation that society forces on its members becomes part of the trap. Because he does not fully understand what is happening to him the alcoholic attempts to hide his drinking, and if he is young and fit he may succeed for quite a long time in fooling his friends or family or employer that he's okay. But as the problem gets worse (as it nearly always does), those closest to him get drawn into a charade. His friends find his company increasingly stressful and tiresome; his wife puts on a brave face to the outside world and plays the martyr at home. But no one will take the bull by the horns and do the one thing that's really necessary – intervene and make him see sense before his alcoholism takes him beyond reach. Because society has told them that drinking is okay, and it is inconceivable that a man or woman close to *them* could have become that rare, miserable creature called an alcoholic. If society, and the education system, had been doing their jobs properly they would have known there were over three quarters of a million registered alcoholics in the country, and only three per cent of them the sort they occasionally see lying under newspapers on the park bench.

## What now?

There are two sets of factors that decide the level of alcohol abuse. One set involves the social, economic and psychological conditions bearing on an individual and that might encourage him to drink. For instance, he will be more likely to drink heavily if his wife has just left him, if he has lost his job, or if he keeps company with a group of hard drinkers. The other set of factors has to do with the availability of alcohol. It doesn't matter how miserable a man or woman may feel: if alcohol isn't available, they won't get drunk.

Motives for drinking are, in the direct sense, beyond the control of government; but government can determine availability. At the very least legislation can be tightened up to prevent under-eighteen-year-olds getting access to drink. Clubs, for instance, should be made accountable for the signing in of under-age drinkers by their members; proof of age, if required, should be a condition of sale at wine stores, and the laws should be changed that make drinking legal for young people if they are either booked in at a hotel, or attend a party in a rented hotel room. In addition, serious consideration should be given to the reduction of drinking hours, especially at clubs, and to the reversal of the present policy which permits food and entertainment licences to be held by drinking establishments.

An equally effective curb on the availability of alcohol, as the Labour Government Think Tank correctly observed, is an increase in price. The objections to it are perfectly well founded: a shrinkage in the market would cut profits to alcohol producers and ultimately cause closures and job losses. The question is, at what price are those profits and jobs being maintained? There's nothing metaphorical in the use of the word 'price'. If we leave aside the matter of thousands of preventable deaths – of innocents as well as addicts – and the misery of broken and unstable homes, we are still left with the increased work-load of the NHS, police and social workers, the lost man-hours through absenteeism and inefficiency, the lost orders consequent on failure to make delivery dates – all of these measured in hard cash.* It's not very far from the truth to say that a successful drinks industry is a financial liability to the nation as a whole.

The cost of the alcohol problem in Britain is being hidden in much the same fashion as the alcoholism of the individual. O'Donnell, at the end of his investigation into the alcohol question, states that three million people are suffering from the catastrophic effects of alcohol abuse. How bad does it have to get, he asks, before anyone will sit up and take notice? The fact is, no one really knows, and no one really cares. But it is worth some careful thought whether in a country that in 1985 spent £250 million promoting alcohol and £1.5 million educating against its abuse, priority should not be given to re-educating people in their attitude to a killer drug.

---

*The influence of alcoholism on industry has moved the Northern Ireland Council on Alcohol to produce a prospectus giving practical guidelines to employers (1986). This step has been endorsed by the CBI, the ICTU, and the Health and Safety Agency.

# 13: The good, the bad, and the alcoholics

Government action is one approach to the alcohol problem, and one that Christians should campaign vigorously to achieve. But it is not a complete solution – after all, in my twenty-five years of drinking I made pretty extensive use of government-backed facilities like the antibuse clinics without shaking the habit. In the end it wasn't clever treatment that saved me, but only God. I needed to be remade from the inside, and that is something no amount of public money will do.

Talk to the average alcoholic, though, and he won't express any more confidence in God than in the hospital that last tried to dry him out. Very likely he will say he tried religion once and found it didn't work, by which he will mean that he went to church for a while, and left when he found no one could wave a magic wand and solve his problem. You might say he should have persevered; but to a great extent I can sympathise with him, because the alcoholic's first encounter with God will not be with the Lord himself but with his church, and in my experience the church's treatment of the drinker leaves much to be desired. Let's be perfectly frank about it. In many cases a church congregation is a cosy little middle class club with a lot to say about social problems and absolutely no inclination to get its hands dirty putting them right. In such a society the alcoholic is *persona non grata*, a distasteful reminder of the other side of life, someone who is so different from respectable church people that the latter are only speaking the literal truth when they object to getting involved on the grounds that they 'wouldn't know what to say.'

But there are other more powerful objections. For instance, it is a widely held belief among Christians that because alcohol is the result of over indulgence, the alcoholic doesn't deserve to be helped. He's made his own bed, and they can't be blamed for letting him lie in it. There is truth in this: whatever the alcoholic may say about his upbringing or situation, responsibility for drinking ultimately lies with him. At the same time, though, it would be naive to claim that an individual can drink (or do anything else) without there being consequences for other, innocent people. If in the terms of the parable Christ can be the naked or starving man, then it is equally certain that he is the alcoholic's wife and children.

The church should help the alcoholic for *their* sake if not for his own. But this objection is cleared away only to reveal a second, for the average Christian will tend to view the alcoholic as a wino, a hard case capable of soaking up hours of attention without reform, and therefore a waste of time. That coping with alcoholics takes time and effort cannot be denied; but to the assertion that it is a waste of time I can only say I'm glad George Averly wasted his time on me, or I wouldn't be here today.

I believe the problem the church has with alcoholism is a crisis of commitment. Say all you like about the cost of ministering to drinkers, in the end the fact is that the ministry can bear fruit, and the reason most people won't take it on is because they don't want to. For many of them it probably raises too many uncomfortable questions about the cocktail cabinet in their living room. You can't go into ministry with alcoholics without first making a careful examination of your own attitude to drink. It would hardly be fair, after all, to pretend to represent a better way of life when you yourself rely more than you should on the occasional (or not so occasional) drink. And this brings us to an important question.

## Should Christians drink?

I'm not hoping here to add anything of substance to a debate that's already been going on for centuries. What I do want is to make sure that this summary of what I see as the Bible's teaching on the matter is fair and true. Both those for and against drinking justify their arguments from scripture, and there is more than a slight temptation to read into it what you want to find, rather than standing under the authority of the biblical writers. So what does the Bible say about drink?

We'll start with something it doesn't say. Nowhere in the Bible does it say that a person should *not* drink alcohol. On the contrary, in the world of the Old Testament, where water was scarce and milk and wine were the main beverages, wine came to symbolise the blessing of God: 'May God give you of heaven's dew and earth's riches,' says Isaac to Jacob, 'and abundance of grain and new wine.' The same thought is expressed in Psalm 104, and in Numbers 15. God had placed wine on the earth for man's use, and he meant it to be enjoyed.

There is no evidence, either, that Jesus disapproved of alcohol. When he turned water into wine at Cana it is not suggested that the wine was non-alcoholic, nor that Jesus himself refrained from drinking it. And at the Last Supper he actually used this alcoholic drink, regularly consumed in excess in the ancient world, to symbolise his own blood. To the strict Pharisees his permissive attitude – his eating and drinking with sinners – was condemned as irreligious, a viewpoint that the Hebrew of Hebrews, Paul, must have shared in his early years. And yet even Paul urged the younger disciple Timothy to break his abstinence, if only for the sake of his sore stomach.

But if the Bible reflects a positive acceptance of the alcohol available in its day, that acceptance is heavily qualified. 'Whoever loves wine and oil will never be rich,' says the writer of Proverbs (21:17). 'Wine is a mocker and beer a brawler; whoever is led astray by them is not wise.' (20:1). Right from the outset, then, the opinion is expressed that over-indulgence in alcohol is not a good thing. Wine might 'gladden the heart of man' (Ps. 104) but its use was forbidden for priests in the service of the altar (Lev. 10:9), and for Nazarites who had taken the vow to refrain (Num. 6:3). And if the early Christians didn't enforce abstinence they made it very clear that drunkenness had no place in Christian behaviour, and that the man who aspired to a position of leadership in the church would be 'not given to much wine' (1 Tim. 3:3).

In the first century AD the conclusion seems to have been that drinking was okay provided it was in moderation. Are we justified in lifting this straight into twentieth century British culture? Many Christians would say yes – life hasn't changed so much as to invalidate the distinction between moderate drinking and inebriation. And anyway Jesus went out of his way to meet people on their own ground, an example which is surely best followed by a Christian presence in the local pub. The problem is, in practice, drinking Christians very rarely use this contact with the world for the sake of the Kingdom.

Certainly I have never heard of anybody being converted through contacts made in a pub; in fact in all my drinking years I never heard God's name used at the bar except as an oath. None of the Christians I knew even dared tell me I was in danger of becoming an alcoholic, let alone witnessed to me. And without the salt of the gospel the presence of Christians in drinking parties can surely only communicate the message that drinking – and drunkenness – is acceptable behaviour. I'm not kidding about that. I know a man in psychiatric hospital who never touched a drink until he saw his minister drinking at a wedding: 'I thought it must be okay, so I took one,' he said. Like me, he wound up as an alcoholic.

Stories like that make me wonder whether drinking Christians are as objective as they like to think they are in their interpretation of scripture. True, as Paul says in Romans 14, a man is free to eat and drink what he likes so long as his conscience is not offended, but he goes on to say that we bear a heavy responsibility for those with weaker consciences than our own. 'It is better not to eat meat or drink wine or to do anything else that will cause your brother to fall' (Rom. 14:21). What conditions were like in Paul's day we can't be sure, but I for one am certain that drinking alcohol – besides carrying the inherent risk of dependency – comes into Paul's category of things that might cause a brother to stumble, and I would hate to think that my indulgence had been another person's downfall. It is not my place to forbid drink to anyone else – each man and woman has, in the end, to make the decision individually. But for me the matter is quite simple: I don't drink. Not because the Bible says I can't (it doesn't) but as a mark of my discipleship, and a way of ensuring that my example doesn't lead anyone else down the dreadful path of alcoholism.

## What the church can do

Assuming then that Christians make a responsible and conscientious decision in their attitude to drink, what aims should the church be pursuing in its fight against alcoholism?

I think we need two reforms. One is to reform our relationship with the young. For too long adult Christians have withdrawn from young people and met the peculiarities of their culture and behaviour—which are often cries for attention—with stern rejection and disapproval. Teenagers need love and education if they are going to stand up to that bombardment of advertising whose principal message is that you can't have fun without alcohol. It's no good just telling them not to drink—that will usually have the effect of driving them to it, as it did with me. They need to be *shown* that life without drink is more fun than life with it. And that means staying close to them as they grow up: loving them; trusting them; crying and laughing with them; and all the time gently pointing them in the direction of the Saviour.

And what about those other teenagers who come to the youth club on motorcycles or hang around street corners kicking beer cans? Are we really helping them if we shut them out of our homes, or if we complain that they've run amok over church premises when the couple of workers we've alotted to oversee them are so overstretched that they can do little more than prevent the building being burned to the ground? I don't think so. Young people aren't an amorphous 'them'—they are individuals, young men and women looking for love and meaning in life, many without jobs, some without family; coping with difficult relationships, loneliness, or the pressure of examinations. And however hard it is to get through to them we must make sure our faith is one with rolled-up sleeves, ready to stand by them and show them, as parents do with their own children, a better way to live.

It is only in this way that we can break the cycle of alcoholism. But educating the young won't help older people who have already come to grief with drink, and here we need a second kind of reform. We must ensure that those who are trying to escape from alcohol dependence find support and friendship in the church. Is it really too much for a church to run a drop-in centre, one small room manned on a rota basis that would allow the alcoholic to sit down and talk and be accepted? It would cost so little; in fact it would begin to justify the colossal expenditure most churches make in rates for the maintenance of a vast building they use only once or twice a week. And I know from my own experience how much difference that could make. The only friends an alcoholic has are the other people at the bar, and if the church isn't willing to offer him friendship – by invitation to a meal or a warm reception at services – he has precious little chance of kicking the habit. It's hard for a drinker to forgive himself. We say blithely that there is forgiveness in God, but all too often our behaviour indicates to the alcoholic not that he is forgiven, but that he has done something that has branded him forever as an incompetent and a failure – exactly those things that, in spite of the assurance he affects when he's drunk, drive him to dependency.

Many Christians will say this is making a mountain out of a molehill. What really matters, they insist, is conversion: get the alcoholic converted and he'll be all right. Well, if nothing else, I hope this book shows that in practice life isn't that simple. Conversion may break the desire for drink, but it will leave intact the complex web of social and emotional problems that caused the drinking. There is no magic wand, only a slow healing. And in that the alcoholic needs every bit of help he can get.

# Other Marshall Pickering Paperbacks

## GOD'S GLOVES: Giving and Receiving Care

*Jennifer Rees-Larcombe*

Jennifer Rees-Larcombe has recently emerged as a significant author on the Christian books scene. GOD'S GLOVES resulted from her growing conviction that the most essential and biblical way of sharing our faith in today's uncaring society is through acts of genuine love and kindness. An outstandingly practical and realistic book, showing how we can overcome personal shyness and fears and use natural opportunities for expressing God's love creatively and sensitively wherever we are.

## THE SACRED DIARY OF ADRIAN PLASS, AGED 37¾

*Adrian Plass, illustrated by Dan Donovan*

A full-length, side-splitting paperback based on the hilarious diary entries, in Christian Family magazine, of Adrian Plass, 'an amiable but somewhat inept' Christian whose wife, Anne, is fortunately understanding and whose teenage son, Gerald, is perceptive and outrageous in equal measure. By his own confession, Adrian 'makes many mistakes and is frequently confused', but despite his own weaknesses and those of his fellow-Christians, which are paraded with the kindest humour, a reassuring sense of belonging to the family of God is the solid, underlying theme. Written by the presenter of TV South's late-night religious programme 'Company'.

## THE SPIRIT IS AMONG US: Personal Renewal and the Local Church

*Philip Hacking*

In this, his robust first book, Philip Hacking (Chairman of the Keswick Convention) contends for the local church as the true centre for revival and spiritual growth. As trendsetting as large celebration gatherings are, there is no substitute, he argues, for a committed Christian life lived in the context of a local fellowship of believers. Nor is there anything as thrilling as seeing the Spirit of God at work daily – developing spiritual depth and maturity in its members and establishing a bridgehead for God to reach the world with his truth. By returning to the New Testament pattern of worship, prayer, preaching and evangelism, Philip Hacking shows how every local church can become a focus for genuine personal renewal.

## ON THE RIGHT TRACK: Contemporary Christians in Sport

*John Searle, foreword by John Motson*

'Killer instinct' is said to get sports stars to the top; but for Christians in sport it is their faith. Thirteen well-known figures from throughout the sporting world reveal here how they manage to combine burning ambition and Christian experience with integrity. Four-times Olympic winner Carl Lewis, ice-skating champion Nicky Slater, and world golf champion Gary Player are amongst them. And the story of the influential organisation Christians in Sport is also told.

If you wish to receive *regular information* about *new books*,
please send your name and address to:

London Bible Warehouse
PO Box 123
Basingstoke
Hants RG23 7NL

Name.................................................................................................

Address ...........................................................................................

.........................................................................................................

.........................................................................................................

.........................................................................................................

I am especially interested in:
- ☐ Biographies
- ☐ Fiction
- ☐ Christian living
- ☐ Issue related books
- ☐ Academic books
- ☐ Bible study aids
- ☐ Children's books
- ☐ Music
- ☐ Other subjects